y him in

Copyright © 2007 illustrations and photographs New Holland Publishers (UK) Ltd
Copyright © 2007 New Holland Publishers (UK) Ltd

ISBN 978 1 84537 484 6
10 9 8 7 6 5 4 3 2 1

Editorial Direction: Rosemary Wilkinson Editor: Anne Konopelski Production: Hazel Kirkman
Designed and created for New Holland by AG&G Books Copyright © 2004 "Specialist" AG&G Books
Design: Glyn Bridgewater Illustrations: Dawn Brend, Gill Bridgewater, Coral Mula and Ann Winterbotham
Editor: Alison Copland Photographs: see page 80
Reproduction by Pica Digital Pte Ltd, Singapore
Printed and bound in Malaysia by Times Offset (M) Sdn. Bhd.

The information in this book is true and complete to the best of our knowledge. All recommendations
are made without guarantee on the part of the authors and the publishers. The authors and publishers
disclaim any liability for damages or injury resulting from the use of this information.

The
PROPAGATION
S[...]

D0406603

The essential guide to raising [...] plants for the home and garden

David Squire
Series editors: A. & G. Bridgewater

NH
NEW
HOLLAND

Contents

Author's foreword

The desire to increase plants is a passion within most gardeners and many methods of propagation are easy and do not need expensive or specialized equipment. Indeed, creating a hardy annual flower border requires only a few packets of seeds, a rake, a draw hoe and a garden line. Layering a low-growing stem from a shrub is also easy, while dividing herbaceous perennials instantly produces several new plants.

A few houseplants are easily and unusually increased, and perhaps none more so than *Chlorophytum comosum* (Spider Plant) and *Saxifraga stolonifera* (Mother of Thousands, Strawberry Geranium), which have plantlets attached to long stems that you can peg into pots of compost. Other houseplants have small plantlets growing on their leaves; you can detach these and press them into compost to encourage the development of roots.

Many plants can be increased in several ways; some are complicated, while others are straightforward, although the development of new plants may not be rapid. Layering, for example, is easy, but rooting takes several months. Throughout this book, where possible the easiest way to increase specific plants is explained.

Part of this practical, all-colour book encompasses an A–Z of popular garden and indoor plants and the ways in which they can be increased. It is arranged alphabetically by current botanical name, but earlier botanical names are included. There is also information about each plant's growth habit – whether annual, biennial, herbaceous, shrub, tree or climber – to enable you to gain a greater understanding as to why a plant is increased in a particular way. The common names index will help you find the right plant quickly. With this easy-to-follow book at your elbow, it becomes possible to increase most plants growing in gardens or indoors.

Measurements

Both metric and imperial measurements are given in this book – for example, 1.8 m (6 ft).

SEASONS

Throughout this book, advice is given about the times of the year to raise new plants. Because of global and even regional variations in climate and temperature, the four main seasons have been used, with each subdivided into 'early', 'mid-' and 'late' – for example, 'early spring', 'mid-spring' and 'late spring'. If you find it helps, these 12 divisions of the year can be applied to the appropriate calendar months in your area.

PLANT NAMES

Currently recommended botanical names for plants are given throughout this book. Where earlier and perhaps better-known botanical names are still used, however, these are included so that you will instantly know the plants being discussed. Common names for plants are also given.

Philosophy of raising plants

Whatever the method you use to increase plants, it is essential when raising them vegetatively (for example, from cuttings and by division) that 'mother plants' are free from pests and diseases, as well as viruses. They should also be good examples of the species being increased. When buying seeds, ensure that they are properly labelled and not excessively old (for most species, the ability to germinate diminishes with increasing age – see page 9).

What are the keys to success?

HELPING NATURE?

Many methods of increasing plants, such as sowing seeds or layering, are only extensions of nature's way to increase plants. Budding and grafting are seldom seen in nature, although stems and branches sometimes rub against each other and become united – but this is a rarity.

When raising plants by seeds sown outdoors, be guided by the weather and the natural cycle of the seasons; it is no good sowing seeds if soil is hard and impervious, saturated with frozen water, or cold and dry. The essential requirements for the germination of seeds are described on page 9.

MAIN WAYS TO INCREASE PLANTS

Seeds
This is the main way in which many plants naturally reproduce and spread themselves. Each seedling usually has the characteristics of its parents, although sometimes they slightly differ. Requirements for germination are moisture, air and warmth. Most seeds also need darkness. Plants raised from seeds (see pages 8–19) include hardy annuals, half-hardy annuals and biennials, and some herbaceous perennials can also be raised in this way.

Layering
It is one of nature's natural ways to increase shrubs with low-growing stems (see page 33). Trees with a pendulous or low habit are further candidates, as well as some climbers. Each new plant is identical to its parent, and it is an easy and popular way to increase plants. However, rooting is not quick, and during the period of rooting it is essential to keep the soil free from weeds and moderately moist. Some plants, such as blackberries and hybrid berries, can be 'tip-layered' by burying the tips of shoots (see page 33).

Wildflower meadows often become a feast of colour from annuals; wildflower mixes are available from seed companies.

Division
Plants with clusters of shoots at their bases, from herbaceous perennials to houseplants such as *Sansevieria trifasciata* (Mother-in-law's Tongue), can be divided. Each new plant closely resembles the parent plant and because each part has roots and stems it soon becomes established (see pages 30–31).

Cuttings
This method of increasing plants produces replicas of the parent plants. Cuttings are formed from leaves, buds and roots; the most popular way is from shoots and stems. The three main forms of cuttings from shoots and stems are softwood, half-ripe (also known as semi-hardwood and semi-mature cuttings) and hardwood (see pages 20–29).

Grafting and budding
These are more complicated methods of increasing plants, and are mainly performed on plants that do not come true from seeds and cannot be divided or layered. Budding involves uniting a bud of the desired variety with a rootstock of known and desired vigour. In grafting, a shoot with several buds is united with a desired rootstock (see pages 38–41).

Plants for easy propagation

Where do I begin?

Many plants can be easily increased by home gardeners and a wide range of them are featured here. Most techniques for increasing plants do not need expensive and complicated equipment, and some methods, such as taking hardwood cuttings, require only a sheltered piece of ground. Layering a shrub is also straightforward and requires just a few simple tools, but rooting takes many months. Grafting and budding are more complex, but still possible.

SINGLE OR MANY PLANTS?

Some methods of increasing plants, such as by seed, produce many new plants, while layering a shrub or tree creates only one new plant for each branch that is layered. Budding and grafting also usually produce just one new plant, although several grafts are used when rejuvenating an old apple tree through methods such as crown grafting.

When new plants are produced from seed, there is a chance that a few of the progeny will differ from the parent plant. With all non-seed methods (cuttings, layers, division, grafts and budding), however, the ensuing plants will be identical to the parent. Softwood cuttings are the most popular type of cutting, used for many soft-stemmed plants.

Annuals

Plants that grow from seed, produce flowers and die within the same year. However, some plants that are normally raised as annuals are not true annuals.

A vibrantly coloured display

Biennials

Plants that are raised from seed, making initial growth one year and flowering in the following one. Some plants raised in this way are not strictly biennial.

Alcea rosea (Hollyhock)

Herbaceous perennials

Usually refers to hardy border plants that die down to ground level in autumn at the end of their growing season, then produce fresh growth in spring.

Medley of herbaceous plants

Roses

Woody and mainly deciduous plants with a permanent framework, regularly pruned to encourage healthier and better growth and the development of flowers.

Rosa 'Paul's Scarlet Climber'

Climbers

Known in North America as vines, climbing plants include a wide range of growing types, including annuals, woody plants and herbaceous perennials.

Vitis (Ornamental Vine)

Shrubs

Woody and perennial, with stems growing from soil level and with no trunk. However, through training, some plants can be grown either as a shrub or as a tree.

Ceanothus thyrsiflorus var. *repens*

Trees

Woody and perennial plants that have a clear trunk between ground level and the lowest branches. They can be evergreen or deciduous, depending on the species.

Amelanchier lamarckii

Soft fruits

These have varied habits, ranging from strawberries that grow at ground level to cane fruits such as raspberries, and bush fruits including gooseberries and black-, red- and whitecurrants.

Redcurrants

Fruit trees

Many fruits grow on trees, including apples, pears, plums, apricots, damsons, cherries, peaches, nectarines, mulberries and quinces.

Apple 'Cox'

Vegetables

These vary both in their growing habits and in the ways in which they are propagated. Most are raised yearly from seed, while others are grown from tubers and a few from bulbs.

Range of lettuces

Culinary herbs

Herbs include a range of plant types: for example, Parsley is a hardy biennial raised as an annual; Sweet Bay is an evergreen shrub; and others are herbaceous perennials.

Herbs in pots

Indoor plants

Plants grown indoors, in greenhouses and in conservatories, range from those raised from seed to those produced from cuttings or by division.

Begonia

Equipment and materials

Depending on the plants you are raising, everything from seed-trays (flats), pots and dibbers (dibbles) to greenhouses and garden frames comes in handy. Increasing woody plants by hardwood cuttings needs only a sheltered piece of land, sharp sand and a spade, and layering a shrub requires just a few pieces of equipment. Sowing half-hardy annuals in late winter and spring needs a greenhouse, a method of heating, seed-trays (flats), compost and a sieve.

TOOLS AND MATERIALS

Once bought – and if regularly cleaned and maintained – many pieces of gardening equipment last for ten or more years. The 'consumable' elements, such as compost, seed-trays (flats) and pots, will, of course, need to be bought more often – perhaps yearly, and usually in late winter or early spring. Compost will also be needed in summer when transferring seedlings and cuttings into pots.

When not in use, place equipment such as propagators and heaters in a dry, well-ventilated shed. Ensure they are clean and dry, then seal them in polythene bags. Check yearly that cables and plugs on electrical equipment have not perished or cracked. Where compost is saved from one year to another, seal the bag's top to prevent it becoming dry and contaminated with pests.

Composts

Several types of compost are available, including loam-based and peat-based varieties.
- Most home gardeners use bags of ready-prepared seed compost when sowing seeds in pots and seed-trays (flats), rather than buying separate ingredients and mixing their own. Never just use garden soil.
- For rooting cuttings, a mixture of equal parts moist peat and sharp sand is best.

Compost

Sieves

You will need a flat-based horticultural sieve, 15–20 cm (6–8 in) wide and 7.5–10 cm (3–4 in) deep, to evenly cover seeds with compost. Alternatively, use a culinary sieve.

Sieve

Seed-trays (flats) and pots

Plastic seed-trays (flats) are essential when you sow half-hardy annual seeds in greenhouses. You will also need pots in a range of sizes – ones 7.5–8 cm (3–3½ in) in diameter are most often used, and both plastic and clay types are available. When seeds are sown in pots, shallow ones, such as Jiffy pots, are useful.

Seed-tray (flat)

Seed-tray with 'cells'

Peat pot

Jiffy pots

Dibber (dibble)

Small plastic dibbers (dibbles), 10–15 cm (4–6 in) long, are useful for transferring seedlings from where they germinated into wider spacings in seed-trays (flats) or into individual pots. Plastic types are easier to keep clean than wooden ones.

Dibber (dibble)

Greenhouses

Heated greenhouses are essential for raising half-hardy annuals (summer-flowering bedding plants) in spring. Several forms are available, including 'even-span', 'lean-to' and 'miniature lean-to', as well as partly glazed sheds. With all of them, good ventilation is essential, as well as adding warmth in late winter and spring. Remember that the larger the greenhouse is, the easier it will be to achieve a uniform and even temperature (but it will also be more expensive to heat).

Mini-type: secure to a wall that is sheltered from wind

Even-span: orientate the ridge east to west

Lean-to: position against a warm, sheltered wall

Glazed shed: orientate the glass towards the sun

TOOLS AND MATERIALS (CONTINUED)

Insulating greenhouses

To reduce heating costs in late winter and spring, when sowing seeds, attach plastic bubble-wrap glazing to the inside of metal or wood greenhouses. Leave space for the ventilator to open and close, and use drawing pins to hold the bubble glazing in place in wooden greenhouses, or special plastic fittings for use in aluminium greenhouses.

Heating a greenhouse

Paraffin (kerosene) heaters: These create warmth and give off moisture that will need to escape through ventilators. They are efficient, but if badly maintained and with a wick that is set too high will produce smoke.

Electric fan heaters: Most have built-in thermostats to ensure that the desired temperature is maintained. Waterproof cables and sockets are essential; avoid hot draughts on plants.

Tubular electric heaters: These are secured to the inside walls and controlled by a thermostat. Ensure that the hot air can rise freely.

Paraffin (kerosene) heater

Electric fan heater

Propagators

Propagators enable seeds to germinate and cuttings to develop roots without heating the entire greenhouse.

Electric propagator: Clean and efficient, but ensure that it has been safely installed for use in a damp environment.

Paraffin (kerosene) propagator: Adaptable and versatile, and can be quickly repositioned within a greenhouse.

Unheated propagator with air vents at top

Garden frame

Cold frames are ideal for acclimatizing ('hardening off') young plants before you plant them in a garden in late spring or early summer. They are unheated and need to be ventilated during warm weather.

Glass jars

Bell jars are traditionally made of glass and put over newly sown seeds and young seedlings to encourage germination and early growth. You can also use glass jam-jars or plastic bottles with their tops cut off.

Bell jar

Plastic bags

When taking softwood cuttings (see pages 20–21), insert short pieces of split canes into the compost and draw a plastic bag over them; secure the bag around the pot with an elastic band.

Border soil

A sheltered corner with friable, well-drained soil creates an ideal nursery bed for plants. It can also be used for hardwood cuttings (see page 22).

Mist propagation units

Professional gardeners have used mist propagation units for many generations to encourage softwood cuttings to develop roots quickly. Small, amateur units are now available. You insert the cuttings in well-drained compost (slightly heated) and the unit regularly covers the leaves with a thin film of water. This keeps the leaves cool and full of moisture until roots develop. The cuttings should then be transferred to small pots.

Always have electrical equipment installed by an experienced and competent electrician.

TIMING

Choosing the right time to increase plants is vital for subsequent success. Seeds are mainly sown in greenhouses in late winter and spring, and outdoors in spring and early summer. Herbaceous perennials are best divided in spring. Softwood cuttings are usually taken in late spring and early summer (when soft shoots are available); half-ripe cuttings (also known as semi-hardwood cuttings) mainly in mid-summer; and hardwood cuttings from mature wood usually in late summer and early autumn, but they can be taken until late winter.

AFTERCARE

After sowing seeds, dividing plants and taking cuttings, care and attention is needed until the new plant is established and growing strongly. Advice on aftercare is given for each method of increasing plants.

Increasing plants from seeds

Are there many types?

There is a wide range of seeds, from dust-like to winged and plumed, and some are fleshy or hard (see below for details and their special needs when sowing). Sowing seeds is the main method of increasing plants, and usually the least expensive. It is often the key to capturing the attention of young children and turning them into gardeners. They are likely then to grow up into people who appreciate plants and respect the environment.

HARVESTING SEEDS

Although most gardeners buy fresh seeds of vegetables, hardy annuals, half-hardy annuals and greenhouse plants each year, some people like to harvest and save seeds from plants that have flowered. However, the plants that result from such seeds can sometimes be variable (gathering seeds is described below). In addition, where a plant is a hybrid – this is indicated by an x between the first (generic) and second (specific) names – its seeds will not breed true to the type; neither will those of varieties that are F1 hybrids (see box on opposite page for the meaning of this term).

TYPES OF SEED

Seeds can be grouped into six main types, and this has an influence on the way they should be sown.

- **Dust-like:** These very fine seeds soon lose their ability to germinate, and therefore are best sown while fresh. They include seeds of *Begonia* and *Meconopsis*. You need only press them into the surface of the compost.
- **Hard-coated:** *Lathyrus odoratus* (Sweet Pea) is an example; crimson and purple-coloured varieties have especially hard-coated seeds. To encourage rapid germination, chip the hard coat with a sharp knife on the side of the seed opposite the 'eye' (a process called 'scarification').
- **Fleshy seeds:** Seeds of some vegetables, such as beans and garden peas, have fleshy seeds; encourage germination by soaking them in water for a day or two before sowing. *Aesculus hippocastanum* (Horse Chestnut), *Castanea sativa* (Sweet Chestnut) and *Quercus* (Oaks) have fleshy seeds.
- **Oily seeds:** These include *Magnolia* seeds, and they soon lose their ability to germinate; you should sow them immediately after gathering.
- **Winged seeds:** Trees such as *Acer pseudoplatanus* (Sycamore), *Fraxinus* (Ash) and *Tilia* (Lime) have winged seeds; you can remove the 'wings' when you are cleaning them, and sow the seeds in the normal way.
- **Plumed seeds:** These include *Erigeron* and *Scabiosa* (Scabious); sometimes, if the plume is still present, they can be difficult to sow at the desired depth.

GATHERING SEEDS

When harvesting seeds, it is essential to choose a dry, sunny day and to keep the seeds of different species separate. The 'parent' plants should be healthy, free from pests and diseases and representative of their kind. Always gather the seedheads or pods before they begin to open. It is better for seedheads and pods to dry out slowly in gentle warmth, rather than quickly in a high temperature.

1 If the whole plant is nearing maturity, you can pull it up, invert it, place it in a thin paper bag and hang it in a dry, airy shed (see left). Alternatively, spread individual seedheads and pods on sheets of paper and place them near a window so that they can ripen in full sun.

2 Once the seedheads are dry, clean the seeds by placing them in a sieve and gently rubbing or tapping (see left). When dry, place them in paper bags or other containers; then label and store them (see opposite page).

HELPING SEEDS TO GERMINATE

Seeds often appear to germinate in the most inhospitable of places, perhaps in cracks between concrete paving slabs and on the tops of walls; seeds of native plants often show this tenacity and adaptability.

Each seed contains an embryo plant, surrounded and protected by a seedcoat and with a source of stored food. Germination is triggered by the presence of moisture, air and warmth, and when these are present germination occurs. Most seeds also need darkness; a few require light.

- **Moisture:** Essential to soften the coats of seeds to enable roots to develop and shoots to push their way upwards through the soil or to the compost's surface. At the onset of germination, a seed absorbs large amounts of water that stimulates growth; roots develop first, then shoots.
- **Air:** All life processes, including germination, need oxygen. To enable oxygen to be available, compost must be well drained to allow air to reach the seeds. There is a desired balance in compost and soil between retaining sufficient moisture and allowing the presence of air; this leads to the practical advice for 'moisture-retentive but well-drained soil or compost'.
- **Warmth:** A suitable temperature is vital to initiate and encourage chemical activity within seeds when moisture and air are present. Seeds vary widely in the optimum temperatures they require. After seeds are liberated from a parent plant, they usually undergo a resting or dormant period that, for many plants, coincides with cold weather, and chilling seeds of some plants will encourage germination (see 'Stratifying seeds', right).
- **Light:** Its influence on germination is variable and many seeds are able to germinate in both light and darkness. However, rather than just leaving seeds on the surface of compost or soil, it is best to sow such seeds at a depth that enables good root development and keeps them moist. The compost or soil also gives the subsequent seedlings a secure base. However, there are some seeds that will only germinate when exposed to light.

VIABILITY OF SEEDS

The ability of a seed to germinate when given suitable conditions (see left) gradually diminishes, and the question many gardeners ask is 'how long will seeds remain viable?' This depends on several factors:

- **Storage:** The best ways to store seeds are described below.
- **Type of plant:** This varies widely; whereas seeds of willows retain viability for only a few days, and those of *Cocos nucifera* (Coconut Palm) only slightly longer, seeds of *Nelumbo nucifera* (Sacred Lotus) are claimed to be viable for more than 100 years.

Usually, it is the viability of vegetable seeds that interests gardeners. Here are indications for a few popular vegetables:

VEGETABLE	VIABILITY	VEGETABLE	VIABILITY
Asparagus	3 years	*Onions*	1 year
Beans	3 years	*Peas*	3 years
Beetroot	4 years	*Peppers*	2 years
Broccoli	5 years	*Pumpkins*	4 years
Cabbages	5 years	*Radishes*	5 years
Carrots	3 years	*Spinach*	5 years
Cauliflowers	5 years	*Squashes*	4 years
Cucumbers	5 years	*Sweetcorn*	2 years
Lettuce	5 years	*Tomatoes*	4 years

Storing seeds

If you are storing seeds gathered from your garden, it is essential first to remove pieces of debris from them; if left, they tend to rot and encourage decay in the seeds. Always collect seeds as soon as they are ripe (see opposite page).

Both home-gathered and bought seeds (that may have been left over from the previous year) can be stored in a dry, dark, airy place with a temperature of 1–5°C (34–41°F). For many gardeners, storing seeds in paper bags in sealed glass or polythene containers in a cool refrigerator is the best solution.

Stratifying seeds

This is a way to encourage seeds to germinate by softening seedcoats and allowing water to enter. It involves soaking the seeds, then chilling them for several weeks to simulate their natural period of dormancy. It is used mainly for large, hard-coated seeds of shrubs and trees, including those of *Amelanchier*, *Cotoneaster*, *Euonymus* and some viburnums. Traditionally, the seeds were put between layers of sharp sand and left outdoors during winter, hence the name 'stratification'.

F1 hybrids

In recent decades, seed companies have offered an increasing number of vegetables and flowers as F1 hybrids. This means that they are a first filial generation, the result of a cross between two pure-bred parents. Their progeny are large, strong and uniform. However, seeds saved from them will not produce replicas of the parents.

Plants to increase from seeds

The majority of wild flowering plants, from those seen in meadows to grasses, increase themselves by means of seeds. They do this naturally and successfully, although not all of the seeds will germinate. Many cultivated plants, however, can be given a more assured start if you take cuttings and root them, or divide established plants. Grafting and budding methods provide plants with roots that have a known vigour and influence on growth.

CHANGING LIFE CYCLES

When raised for growing in gardens or as plants for home decoration, many seed-raised plants grown in temperate climates have a different growth pattern or life cycle from their natural one. For example, *Lobelia erinus* (Edging Lobelia) is a half-hardy perennial usually grown as a half-hardy annual; *Mirabilis jalapa* (Marvel of Peru) is a perennial grown as a half-hardy annual; and *Impatiens walleriana* (Busy Lizzie) is a greenhouse perennial invariably grown as a half-hardy annual. *Bellis perennis* (Daisy) and *Dianthus barbatus* (Sweet William) are perennials grown as biennials. The purpose of changing the cycle of growth of such plants is to produce many plants at the same time, in the easiest way possible.

WHEN TO SOW

The life cycle of plants, from hardy annuals to half-hardy annuals, biennials and hardy herbaceous perennials, influences when and how you should sow them:

Hardy annuals

Sow mainly during mid- and late spring (see pages 12–13). Their range is wide and you can easily create medleys, including a yellow border fronted by yellow annual lupins and backed by tall sunflowers.

Agrostemma githago 'Milas'

Half-hardy annuals

Sow mainly in late winter and spring in greenhouses in gentle warmth (see pages 18–19). A traditional medley is *Begonia semperflorens* (Wax Begonia), *Lobelia erinus* (Edging Lobelia) and *Lobularia maritima* (Sweet Alyssum).

Petunia x *hybrida*

Hardy biennials

Sow in a nursery bed in spring and early summer (see pages 14–15). For extra colour, combine spring-flowering bulbs such as tulips with the popular biennials *Bellis perennis* (Common Daisy) and *Myosotis sylvatica* (Forget-me-not).

Dianthus barbatus

Hardy herbaceous perennials

Sow in nursery beds in spring and early summer (see pages 14–15). Seed catalogues abound with herbaceous perennials that can be raised from seeds, including *Achillea* (Yarrow), *Dictamnus albus* (Burning Bush) and *Echinacea purpurea* (Purple Cone Flower).

Coreopsis verticillata

Shrubs and trees

Sow seeds of shrubs and trees at any time of year. As their seeds usually have tough coats, they need to be stratified (see page 9). Alternatively, chip or sandpaper them to improve their chances of germination.

Cistus x *dansereaui*

Climbers

Lathyrus odoratus (Sweet Pea)

Many climbers are increased from cuttings or layered stems, but a few can be raised from seeds, including *Lathyrus latifolius* (Everlasting Sweet Pea), *Lathyrus odoratus* (Sweet Pea) and *Tropaeolum peregrinum* (Canary Creeper).

Palms

Fresh seeds and high temperatures, up to 35°C (95°F), are usually needed to encourage germination. However, an easier way is to mix seeds with moist peat and place them in a strong, clear, polythene bag. Seal the bag and put it in a warm, shaded greenhouse, perhaps under the staging. When roots and leaves appear, transfer the seedlings into individual pots.

What is germination?

To most gardeners, germination is when young shoots appear above the surface of the soil in the garden or compost in seed-trays (flats) and pots in greenhouses. Technically, however, germination is when the embryo within a seed breaks into growth, initiating the development of shoots and roots. The requirements for germination – moisture, air and warmth, together with the influence of light – are described on page 9.

Vegetables

Lettuce 'Buttercrunch'

Most vegetables are grown from seeds (see pages 16–17). Many, such as peas, lettuces, beetroot and spring onions (scallions), should be sown where they will germinate and grow until harvested. Others, including Brussels sprouts and cabbages, should be sown in seed beds; later, the young plants should be transferred to their growing positions.

SOWING VERY FINE SEEDS

Fine, dust-like seeds, such as those of *Begonia* and *Meconopsis*, are difficult to see and handle; although you can just press them onto the surface of the compost, often it is better to mix them with dry silver sand and then sow them.

Here are a few clues to success when sowing fine seeds:

- Select a dry, shallow pot, about 13 cm (5 in) wide, and fill it with soil-based seed compost (this has a finer texture than peat-based types and forms a flatter surface for fine seeds).
- Firm the compost evenly with your fingers, then refill and level it with the pot's surface. Use a round compost presser (or the top of a jar) to level the surface about 12 mm (½ in) below the rim.
- Open the seed packet and add a heaped teaspoon of silver sand to the packet. Close the packet and shake to ensure the contents are well mixed.
- Some gardeners sow seeds directly from the packet, but unless you are experienced at this it is likely that all of the seeds will fall out in a heap.
- Instead, tip the mixture of seeds and silver sand into a piece of white, stiff, paper or card – about 15 cm (6 in) long and 6 cm (2½ in) wide – that has been folded into a V-shape along its length. Then you can easily see the mixture of seeds and silver sand, and by directing the folded paper over the compost and tapping its end you can encourage the seeds to fall over the surface evenly.
- There is no need to cover the seeds; just use a presser, or the top of a jar, to press them into the compost.
- Stand the pot in a bowl shallowly filled with water; when moisture seeps to the surface of the compost, remove the pot and allow it to drain. Then, either cover it with a transparent lid or place the pot in a polythene bag and seal it.
- Remove the bag as soon as seedlings appear.

Culinary herbs

Petroselinum crispum (Parsley)

A few culinary herbs, such as *Allium sativum* (Garlic) and *Allium schoenoprasum* (Chives), are bulbous and are easily increased by division. Others, such as *Anethum graveolens* (Dill), *Anthriscus cerefolium* (Chervil), *Carum carvi* (Caraway), *Ocimum basilicum* (Sweet Basil), *Origanum majorana* (Sweet Marjoram), *Petroselinum crispum* (Parsley) and *Satureja hortensis* (Summer Savory), are usually raised from seeds. These and other culinary herbs are featured in the A–Z (see pages 42–78).

Hardy annuals in borders

Is there a wide range?

There are many hardy annuals to grow in gardens (see opposite page). You simply sow the seeds where they will germinate, grow and flower, either in borders totally dedicated to annuals or as fillers in established herbaceous or mixed borders. When growing them in dedicated borders, sow the seeds in groups of differing final plant sizes, so that they dovetail with each other and drench the bed or border in inexpensive colour throughout summer.

WHEN SHOULD I SOW THEM?

It is a waste of seeds and time to sow hardy annuals too early in spring, when the soil is still cold and wet; the seeds will not germinate and may even decay before conditions are right for germination.

Here are a few clues to sowing hardy annuals:
• The earliest time for sowing seeds depends on the weather, and even within a distance of a hundred miles the optimum time may vary by seven to ten days – sometimes more. If you are in doubt about a suitable time, your local gardening club will be able to help.
• Gardens on warm, sun-facing slopes can be sown earlier than those with a cold and wind-blown aspect.
• While waiting for the soil to warm up and dry out slightly, avoid walking on it and causing compaction.
• Wait until the soil's surface is dry and crumbly – usually during mid- and late spring.

HOW TO SOW HARDY ANNUALS IN BORDERS

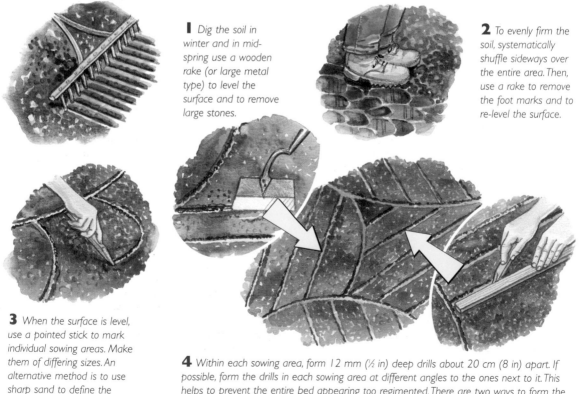

1 Dig the soil in winter and in mid-spring use a wooden rake (or large metal type) to level the surface and to remove large stones.

2 To evenly firm the soil, systematically shuffle sideways over the entire area. Then, use a rake to remove the foot marks and to re-level the surface.

3 When the surface is level, use a pointed stick to mark individual sowing areas. Make them of differing sizes. An alternative method is to use sharp sand to define the sowing areas. Make corner areas large and dominant.

4 Within each sowing area, form 12 mm (½ in) deep drills about 20 cm (8 in) apart. If possible, form the drills in each sowing area at different angles to the ones next to it. This helps to prevent the entire bed appearing too regimented. There are two ways to form the drills: using a draw hoe (above left) and with a pointed stick guided by another stick (above right). Using a straight stick for guidance is ideal when sowing a small area.

HOW TO SOW HARDY ANNUALS IN BORDERS (CONTINUED)

5 Sow seeds evenly and thinly in the base of each drill. Label each sowing area with the name of the annual, together with the date.

6 Use the flat top of a metal rake to push and pull friable soil over the seeds. Then, employ the top of the rake again to tap down and firm soil over the drills.

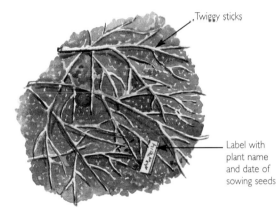

Twiggy sticks

Label with plant name and date of sowing seeds

7 When sowing is complete, lightly but thoroughly water the entire area without disturbing the seeds (use an upturned fine rose). Then, to prevent birds disturbing the surface, either lay twiggy sticks over the area, or stretch black cotton over the drills (but ensure that birds cannot become entangled in it). As soon as seeds germinate, remove the twiggy sticks or lines of cotton.

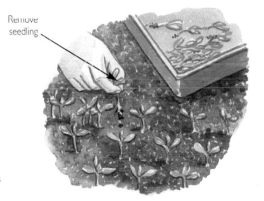

Remove seedling

8 When the seedlings are large enough to handle, carefully thin them without unduly disturbing the soil and loosening the roots of the remaining seedlings. Put the seedlings that are removed on a compost heap; do not leave them on the soil's surface. Then, lightly but thoroughly water the whole area.

ANNUALS TO SOW IN THIS WAY

The range of hardy annuals that can be sown in borders each year is extremely wide, and all of the following plants are described in the 'A–Z of propagating plants' (see pages 42–78):

- *Agrostemma githago* 'Milas' (Corn Cockle)
- *Amaranthus caudatus* (Love-lies-Bleeding)
- *Calendula officinalis* (Pot Marigold)
- *Chrysanthemum carinatum* (Annual Chrysanthemum)
- *Clarkia elegans* (Clarkia)
- *Clarkia pulchella* (Clarkia)
- *Consolida ajacis* (Larkspur)
- *Convolvulus tricolor*
- *Eschscholzia californica* (Californian Poppy)
- *Gypsophila elegans* (Baby's Breath)
- *Helianthus annuus* (Sunflower)
- *Hibiscus trionum* (Flower-of-an-hour)
- *Iberis umbellata* (Candytuft)
- *Lavatera trimestris* (Annual Mallow)
- *Limnanthes douglasii* (Poached Egg Plant)
- *Linaria maroccana* (Toadflax)
- *Linum grandiflorum* 'Rubrum' (Scarlet Flax)
- *Linum usitatissimum* (Common Flax)
- *Lobularia maritima* (Sweet Alyssum)
- *Lychnis viscaria* (Annual Campion)
- *Malcolmia maritima* (Virginia Stock)
- *Matthiola bicornis* (Night-scented Stock)
- *Nigella damascena* (Love-in-a-mist)
- *Papaver rhoeas* (Field Poppy)
- *Papaver somniferum* (Opium Poppy)
- *Reseda odorata* (Mignonette)
- *Rudbeckia hirta* (Black-eyed Susan)
- *Scabiosa atropurpurea* (Sweet Scabious)

Biennials and herbaceous perennials

Are these long-term plants?

Biennials are plants that flower in their second year of growth. In gardens, they are sown in spring and early summer for flowering during the following year, when they are usually discarded after they cease flowering. However, many biennials are actually perennial in nature, and will continue growing and reseeding themselves. Herbaceous perennials, once planted, have life-spans of 3–5 years before they become congested and need to be divided.

WHEN SHOULD I SOW?

You can sow both hardy biennials and herbaceous perennials in seed beds outdoors, later transplanting the young plants to their growing positions in beds and borders. Their sowing and transplanting times differ slightly, however.

Hardy biennials
- Sow seeds in drills in a nursery bed in spring and early summer. Always sow seeds evenly and thinly.
- Thin seedlings slightly when they are large enough to handle. If necessary, refirm soil around those that remain. Then lightly but thoroughly water the soil.
- In autumn of the same year, or early spring of the following one, transfer plants to their growing position.

Herbaceous perennials
- Sow seeds in drills in a nursery bed in spring and early summer, later thinning them to wider spacings and subsequently planting them in a nursery bed. During spring or early summer of the following year, plant them in borders. After planting, thoroughly water the soil.
- Alternatively, sow seeds in shallow pots in spring and early summer and place them in a cold frame; this encourages more rapid germination and prevents compost becoming excessively wet, causing seeds to rot.
- A further choice is to sow seeds in seed-trays (flats) in spring and early summer and to place them in a cold or slightly warm greenhouse. Later, plant them in a nursery bed.

SOWING BIENNIALS AND HERBACEOUS PERENNIALS

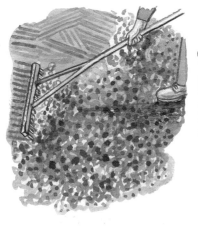

1 During winter, dig a seed bed in a sheltered part of a garden and remove perennial weeds. In early spring, use a wooden rake (or a large metal type) to level the surface and break it to a fine tilth. If the soil is stony, do not rake off all stones as they help prevent compaction.

2 To firm the surface evenly, shuffle sideways over the entire surface. As well as consolidating the soil, this helps to break down large lumps. Do not use a garden roller, because it makes the surface uneven. Additionally, if the soil is damp its use results in clods of soil on the surface.

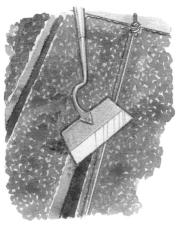

3 Use short canes to mark the ends of each row and stretch a garden line between them. Then, use the edge of a draw hoe to form a shallow drill, 6–12 mm (¼–½ in) deep. Remove the garden line before sowing seeds. Take care not to knock soil into the drill.

SOWING BIENNIALS AND HERBACEOUS PERENNIALS (CONTINUED)

4 Sow seeds evenly and thinly in the bases of the drills. Congested seedlings are susceptible to diseases, and this also creates unnecessary competition for water, air and nutrients. Stand on a board to avoid compacting unsown soil.

5 Cover the seeds either by straddling the row and shuffling forward to guide friable soil over the seeds (above), or by using the flat top of a metal rake to push and pull soil over the seeds. Firm the surface by using your feet or the flat top of a metal rake.

6 Label the ends of the rows and lightly draw a metal rake over the rows (in the direction of the rows and not across) to remove footprints and level the soil's surface. This prevents water resting in puddles on the surface.

Biennials to raise in this way

- *Alcea rosea* (Hollyhock)
- *Bellis perennis* (Common Daisy)
- *Dianthus barbatus* (Sweet William)
- *Digitalis purpurea* (Foxglove)
- *Erysimum x allionii* (Siberian Wallflower)
- *Erysimum alpinum* (Alpine Wallflower)
- *Erysimum cheiri* (Wallflower)
- *Myosotis sylvatica* (Forget-me-not)

Herbaceous perennials to raise in this way

- *Acanthus mollis* (Bear's Breeches)
- *Acanthus spinosus* (Bear's Breeches)
- *Achillea* (Yarrow)
- *Campanula* (some species)
- *Centaurea* (some species)
- *Dictamnus albus* (Burning Bush)
- *Echinacea purpurea* (Purple Cone Flower)
- *Incarvillea delavayi*
- *Leucanthemum maximum* (syn. *Chrysanthemum maximum*; Shasta Daisy)
- *Lupinus polyphyllus* (but not named varieties)
- *Sisyrinchium*

THINNING SEEDLINGS

Thinning seedlings provides the ones that remain with more space. If left, they become congested, thin and weak.

- Thin seedlings as soon as they are large enough to handle.
- Do not leave pulled up seedlings on the surface of the soil.
- Check that soil is not loosened around remaining seedlings; if necessary, firm soil around them.
- When thinning is complete, lightly but thoroughly water the soil's surface. This may need to be repeated.

Thinning seedlings enables those that remain to grow more strongly and to be less susceptible to diseases.

TRANSPLANTING SEEDLINGS

Instead of thinning seedlings, leave them to grow slightly larger and then transplant to wider spacings in nursery beds.

- Water both the seed bed and nursery bed a day before moving the seedlings.
- Carefully fork up the young plants without unnecessarily damaging the roots. Do not allow their roots to become dry.
- Replant them, with soil firmed around their roots.
- Lightly but thoroughly water the soil.

Sowing vegetable seeds

What is the best method?

Many vegetable seeds are best sown in V-shaped drills about 12 mm (½ in) deep for most seeds, although larger ones, such as those of French beans, need drills that are about 5 cm (2 in) deep (see below for desired depths for specific vegetables). Seedlings in a V-shaped drill, which produces a narrow row, will usually require thinning (see below). A few vegetables, such as garden peas, can be sown in flat-bottomed trenches; this enables a broad row to be created.

SUCCESS WITH VEGETABLE SEEDS

There are five main clues to success with vegetable seeds:
- Form drills that are uniformly deep and at the correct depth for the vegetable being sown. If too deep, the seeds will not germinate; if too shallow, the seedlings will not be properly established.
- Sow seeds evenly and thinly. There is no advantage in sowing seeds thickly (often just to use up a packet).
- Cover seeds to a uniform depth.
- Thin seedlings to ensure the remaining ones are healthy.
- After sowing, keep the soil moist but not waterlogged.

SOWING SEEDS IN V-SHAPED DRILLS

1 *In winter, dig the soil. In spring, evenly firm the soil by systematically treading over it (see page 14) and rake it level.*

2 *Stretch a garden line between two short canes and use a draw hoe to form an evenly deep drill (see below for depths).*

3 *Remove the garden line and sow seeds evenly and thinly in the drill's base (see opposite for sowing preferences).*

ALTERNATIVE WAYS TO COVER AND FIRM SEEDS

Use the flat top of a metal rake to draw and push soil over the seeds.

Firm the surface with the flat top of a metal rake; then lightly draw the rake over the row (in the direction of the row) to ensure it is level.

4 *To cover the drill, straddle the row and slowly shuffle forward so that friable soil is pushed over the seeds. Then firm the soil by carefully walking over it. Label the ends of the rows, and shallowly draw a metal rake over the row (in the direction of the rows and not across them) to remove footprints and level the soil's surface.*

Vegetables to sow in this way
- **Broad (fava) beans:** drills 7.5 cm (3 in) deep; sow seeds 23 cm (9 in) apart.
- **French beans:** drills 5 cm (2 in) deep; sow seeds 7.5–10 cm (3–4 in) apart.
- **Runner beans:** drills 5 cm (2 in) deep; sow seeds 15 cm (6 in) apart.
- **Beetroot:** drills 2.5 cm (1 in) deep; sow seeds in clusters of three, 10–15 cm (4–6 in) apart. Later, thin to one strong seedling at each position.
- **Brussels sprouts and cabbages:** drills 12–18 mm (½–¾ in) deep in a seed bed, for later planting in growing positions.
- **Carrots:** drills 12–18 mm (½–¾ in) deep; sow thinly and later thin.
- **Lettuce:** drills 12 mm (½ in) deep; sow thinly and later thin the seedlings.
- **Parsnips:** drills 12–18 mm (½–¾ in) deep; sow clusters of three seeds about 15 cm (6 in) apart and later thin to one strong seedling at each position.
- **Radishes:** drills 12 mm (½ in) deep; thin seedlings to about 2.5 cm (1 in) apart.
- **Spinach:** drills 12–18 mm (½–¾ in) deep; later, thin seedlings.
- **Spring onions (scallions):** drills 12 mm (½ in) deep; thinning is not necessary.
- **Turnips:** drills 12–18 mm (½–¾ in) deep; thin seedlings.

FLAT-BOTTOMED TRENCHES

Garden peas are ideal for sowing in trenches, although sometimes they are sown in two drills, 7.5 cm (3 in) deep and 20 cm (8 in) apart. However, it is easier to use a flat-bottomed trench, 6.5 cm (2¾ in) deep and 20 cm (8 in) wide.

On the base of the trench, position three rows of peas, 7.5 cm (3 in) apart, across the trench's width and 5 cm (2 in) apart in the rows. Stagger the positions of seeds within the rows so that each seedling has the maximum amount of space. There is no need to thin the seedlings.

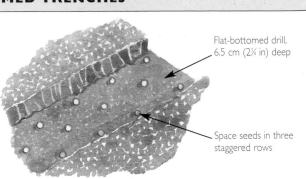

Flat-bottomed drill, 6.5 cm (2¾ in) deep

Space seeds in three staggered rows

PLANTING POTATO TUBERS (SEED POTATOES)

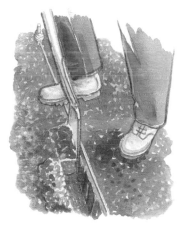

1 Potatoes are raised from tubers saved from the previous year's crop and known as 'seed' potatoes. They are planted during mid- and late spring. Use a spade to form 15 cm (6 in) drills that are uniformly deep.

2 Place seed potatoes in the base of the drill, 30 cm (12 in) apart for early crops and 40 cm (16 in) for main crops. Position the tubers with their 'eyes' (buds) facing upwards. Take care not to damage either the eyes or any small shoots.

3 Use a draw hoe to pull friable soil (from both sides of the row) over the tubers so that it forms a long, continuous mound 10–15 cm (4–6 in) high over the tubers. As the shoots grow, further 'earthing up' of the rows will be required.

SOWING PREFERENCES

When sowing seeds in V-shaped drills, there are three main options, depending on the seed and its size:
- **Continuous line:** Usual way to sow small seeds, such as those of carrots, lettuces, onions, radishes, spinach and turnips. For information about thinning the seedlings, see opposite page.
- **Singly spaced:** Space individual seeds at intervals along the drill. Used for broad (fava) beans, French beans and runner beans. Garden peas are also treated this way when grown in V-shaped drills.
- **In clusters:** Sow seeds in clusters (usually formed of three seeds) along the drill. Later, thin the seedlings to just one in each position.

Fluid sowing

Seeds are mixed with a gel, often wallpaper paste, and squeezed out of a small hole made in the corner of a plastic bag into the base of a V-shaped drill. The gel helps to retain moisture around the seeds and encourages even and rapid germination.

Sowing seeds in a greenhouse

What equipment is needed?

You will need a means of providing warmth, usually 16–21°C (61–70°F), in the greenhouse. A strong bench to support sown seed-trays (flats), compost that retains moisture and allows air penetration, a soil presser (to firm the compost uniformly) and a horticultural sieve will also be necessary. Propagation cases, which are heated by electricity or paraffin (kerosene), are a bonus and will enable the greenhouse's general temperature to be lowered.

SEEDS TO SOW IN GREENHOUSES

Many plants for the garden and home are raised in gentle warmth in greenhouses. For details of individual plants, see the A–Z of propagating plants (pages 42–78).

- **Half-hardy annuals (for later planting into beds and borders):** These are sometimes known as summer-flowering bedding plants and include *Begonia semperflorens* (Wax Begonia), *Lobelia erinus* (Edging Lobelia) and *Lobularia maritima* (Sweet Alyssum).

- **Indoor flowering pot plants:** These are plants for home decoration, including *Calceolaria* x *herbeohybrida* (Slipper Plant), *Primula malacoides* (Fairy Primrose) and *Pericallis* x *hybrida* (Florist's Cineraria).
- **Culinary herbs:** There is a wide range to choose from, including *Ocimum basilicum* (Sweet Basil), *Origanum majorana* (Sweet Marjoram) and *Myrrhis odorata* (Sweet Cicely). Some herbs can also be sown outdoors.

SOWING SEEDS IN SEED-TRAYS (FLATS) IN A GREENHOUSE

Greenhouses provide assured warmth in which seeds can germinate and young seedlings grow healthily. After germination, transfer the seedlings ('pricking off' – see opposite page) to wider spacings in seed-trays (flats). Later, plants for decorating homes need to be moved to individual pots (also see opposite page). Always use pest and disease-free compost. Using clean and dry seed-trays is also essential.

1 *Fill a seed-tray (flat) with fresh compost and use your fingers to firm it, especially around the edges. Then refill with compost.*

2 *Run a straight piece of wood over the top of the tray to remove any excess. Then use a compost presser to firm the surface to 12 mm (½ in) below the rim.*

3 *Tip a few seeds onto a piece of stiff, folded paper; tap the end to spread the seeds evenly over the compost surface, but not near the edges.*

4 *Use a flat-based horticultural sieve to cover the seeds with compost to 3–4 times their thickness. Alternatively, use a culinary sieve, as shown here.*

5 *To water the compost, stand the seed-tray in a flat-based bowl shallowly filled with water. Remove when the surface is moist. Then cover the tray as described on the opposite page.*

PRICKING OFF SEEDLINGS

As soon as the seedlings are large enough to handle, they must be transferred ('pricked off') so that each has more space in which to develop, and an increase in light and air. Seedlings left clustered together become weak and etiolated, and more susceptible to diseases than those with a good circulation of air around them. It is better to transfer seedlings when young, rather than leaving them until large, tough and tightly clustered.

1 *After germination, remove the cover. Whenever the compost shows signs of drying out, water the seedlings by standing the seed-tray (flat) in a bowl shallowly filled with water (see opposite page).*

2 *When the seedlings are large enough to handle, water them from below. Then use a small fork to lift a few seedlings and place them on damp newspaper.*

3 *Fill and firm the compost in another seed-tray. Use a small dibber (dibble) to make holes, keeping the outer row 12 mm (½ in) from the sides of the tray.*

4 *Hold a seedling by one of its leaves and insert the roots into a hole (to the same depth as before). Gently firm the compost around the seedlings.*

5 *When the seed-tray is full, gently tap the tray's edges to level any loose compost. Water carefully from above to settle the compost around the roots. Then proceed as described below.*

COVERING THE SEED-TRAY (FLAT)

After you have sown the seeds, the tray (flat) needs to be covered to prevent the surface of the compost drying out. There are a couple of ways of doing this:

- The traditional method is to place a piece of glass over the seed-tray (flat). However, because condensation forms on the underside, you must wipe the glass clear each morning, then invert it so that the dry side is facing the compost. To create a dark environment (this is needed by most seeds to aid germination), place some newspaper on top of the glass.

- More recently, transparent plastic 'lids' that fit seed-trays have been produced, and these are ideal where children might approach the seedlings and cut themselves on the glass. Again, cover with newspaper (see right).

To create darkness, cover the glass or plastic lid with newspaper

CARE OF YOUNG PLANTS

After pricking off the seedlings, keep the compost lightly moist. When leaves touch, plants to be grown as summer-flowering bedding plants can be acclimatized to outdoor conditions, then planted in beds when all risk of frost has passed.

Plants to be grown as houseplants will need repotting, as described below.

1. Water the compost. When drained, use a small fork to remove the plants.
2. Fill a clean pot with potting compost and lightly firm. Hold a plant by its stem and check that it is at the same depth as before (see the dark line on the stem); trickle and firm the compost around the roots.
3. Add and firm further compost; check the surface is 12 mm (½ in) below the pot's rim. Water the compost from above and place in gentle warmth until established.

Softwood cuttings

What are softwood cuttings?

These cuttings are taken from soft young shoots, before they show any sign of hardening. This is the normal method used for increasing chrysanthemums, many houseplants, perennials and sub-shrubs. You can take softwood cuttings throughout the year from plants that are actively growing in warm greenhouses, but only during early and mid-summer from outdoor plants. It is essential that the shoots you select are still soft; otherwise the cuttings are less likely to form roots.

THE IDEAL CUTTING

- Must be full of moisture, not dry and shrivelled. Therefore, the day before taking a cutting, water the parent plant.
- Should usually be 5–7.5 cm (2–3 in) long, although cuttings with wide spaces between their leaf-joints are invariably longer. The optimum size of a cutting depends on the plant, but always avoid long, thin ones, or very small ones.
- Should be taken from a non-flowering shoot, with a growth bud at its top rather than a flower bud.
- Must be typical of its species and free from all kinds of pests and diseases. If a plant is infested with aphids, or any other sap-sucking insect, there is a chance that viruses will have been transmitted to it.

TAKING A STEM-TIP CUTTING

Always cut the stem cleanly, without leaving a ragged end

Trimming a cutting is best carried out on a firm, wooden surface

1 *Water the plant the day before taking cuttings. Use scissors or a sharp knife to remove a shoot, severing it just above a leaf-joint. This prevents small stubs being left at a shoot's base.*

2 *Use a sharp knife and cut the shoot immediately below a leaf-joint, leaving a shoot 5–7.5 cm (2–3 in) long. Cut off the lower leaves. Pick up and compost old leaves and shoots.*

3 *Fill a shallow pot with equal parts moist peat and sharp sand; firm it to 12 mm (½ in) below the rim. Use a small dibber (dibble), to form a hole 18–25 mm (¾–1 in) deep) and about 12 mm (½ in) from the pot's side. Insert the cutting and firm compost around it. Several cuttings can be inserted in a pot. Add a label and gently water the compost with a spray of water from an upturned rose. Insert four or five short split canes into the compost around the pot's edge and draw a clear polythene bag over the top. This creates a humid atmosphere around the cuttings. Seal it around the pot with an elastic band. Place in gentle warmth, perhaps on a shaded window but avoiding strong and direct sunlight. Alternatively, place in a greenhouse. When young shoots develop from the leaf-joints, remove the bag and, after a week or so, transfer the cuttings to individual pots.*

Rooting *Impatiens walleriana* (Busy Lizzie) in water

Cuttings of *Impatiens walleriana* will root when suspended by a piece of stiff card over a glass of water. When roots form, transfer the cutting to compost in a pot. Until the newly rooted cutting is established, place the pot in slight shade.

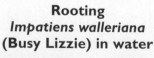

ROOTING A SAINTPAULIA IN WATER

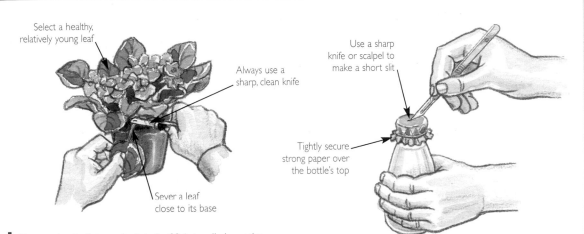

Select a healthy, relatively young leaf

Always use a sharp, clean knife

Sever a leaf close to its base

Use a sharp knife or scalpel to make a short slit

Tightly secure strong paper over the bottle's top

1 *Encouraging leaf-stems (petioles) of* Saintpaulia ionantha *(African Violet) to form roots is an ideal way to increase these superb houseplants. Such cuttings are known as leaf-petiole cuttings and are formed of a piece of stem and a leaf. Instead of inserting leaf-stems in compost, you suspend them in water. The day before taking leaf-petiole cuttings, water the parent plant to ensure its leaves and stems are full of water. Select a healthy plant and use a sharp knife to sever the stem close to its base. You can take several cuttings from the same plant.*

2 *Wash and clean a small glass bottle or similar container and fill with clean water to about 18 mm (¾ in) below the top. Then, tightly pull a piece of strong paper over the top, securing it to the sides with an elastic band. Use a sharp, pointed knife (or scalpel) to form a short slit. The stem, when inserted, must fit tightly to prevent it moving. Trim off excess paper from the 'lid'.*

INCREASING PELARGONIUMS FROM SOFTWOOD CUTTINGS

Pelargoniums (shrub-like plants mainly native to South Africa) should not be confused with garden geraniums, which are hardy and herbaceous. In temperate climates, pelargoniums are grown as houseplants, as well as filling beds and containers with colour outdoors during summer. A popular and easy way to increase zonal, ivy-leaved and scented-leaved pelargoniums is from cuttings:

- In late summer or early autumn, select a healthy plant and water the compost.
- The following day, sever a non-flowering shoot just above a leaf-joint so that it is 15–20 cm (6–8 in) long; this ensures that a short stub of stem is not left on the parent plant.
- Use a sharp knife to trim the cutting about 10 cm (4 in) long, cutting just below a leaf-joint. Also trim off the lower leaf close to the stem.
- Fill and lightly firm a mixture of equal parts moist peat and sharp sand in a 10–13 cm (4–5 in) wide pot; insert 3–4 cuttings, 3.5–5 cm (1½–2 in) deep, in it, but not touching the sides. The lowest leaf on each cutting should be slightly above the compost's surface.
- Water the compost and keep at 10°C (50°F) throughout the winter. When roots appear, transfer each cutting to an individual pot.
- You should always ensure that pelargoniums are not exposed to frost. Therefore, do not be in a hurry to plant them in beds and containers in early summer.

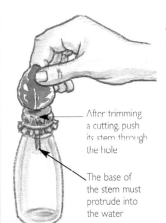

After trimming a cutting, push its stem through the hole

The base of the stem must protrude into the water

3 *Trim the stem to about 3.5 cm (1½ in) long and push it through the hole in the top, so that it descends 6–12 mm (¼–½ in) into the water. Place in gentle warmth and slight shade; regularly check to make sure the stem's base is covered. When roots form, carefully remove the cutting and transfer it to a small pot filled with compost.*

HORMONE ROOTING POWDER

Used for many years, this powder encourages cuttings to form roots quickly, before they decay. After preparing the cuttings (trimming to size, cutting the bases just below a leaf-joint and removing the lower leaves), dip the ends in hormone rooting powder and then insert them in well-drained but moisture-retentive compost.

Most hormone rooting powders contain a fungicide that helps to prevent diseases entering cuttings before they form roots. Wash your hands after touching these powders.

Half-ripe and hardwood cuttings

How do these differ?

Half-ripe cuttings – also known as semi-hardwood, semi-ripe and semi-mature cuttings – are taken from a parent plant in mid- and late summer. The wood needs to be firm, but less mature than for hardwood cuttings. Hardwood cuttings are taken in autumn, mainly from deciduous shrubs but sometimes from evergreens. If the shrub is deciduous, wait until all the leaves fall off. Some shrubs, such as *Philadelphus* (Mock Orange), can be increased by both half-ripe and hardwood cuttings.

HALF-RIPE CUTTINGS

How long before roots form? After taking cuttings and inserting them in pots, place them in a sun-sheltered cold frame. Regularly check that the compost is evenly moist. By the following spring, the cuttings will have developed roots; plant them in a nursery bed until autumn, when they are large enough to plant in a border.

1 Take half-ripe cuttings when shoots are firmer than for softwood cuttings, but less mature than hardwood cuttings. Remove 10–15 cm (4–6 in) long shoots, preferably with a small piece of the older main stem attached to their bases.

2 Remove the lower leaves and trim the cutting's base, cutting off any whisker-like growths from around the older piece of wood (known as a 'heel'). Not all half-ripe cuttings have heels, but when present they encourage rapid rooting.

3 Dip the base of each cutting in hormone rooting powder, and insert them 3.5–5 cm (1½–2 in) deep in pots containing equal parts moist peat and sharp sand. Position each cutting 12–18 cm (½–¾ in) from the pot's edge. Firm and water the compost.

Shrubs to increase in this way
• *Arctostaphylos* • *Aucuba*
• *Berberis* • *Brachyglottis*
• *Bupleurum* • *Callistemon*
• *Camellia* • *Carpenteria*
• *Ceanothus* (some)
• *Cytisus* (some)
• *Deutzia* • *Elaeagnus*
• *Garrya elliptica*
• *Ilex (some)*
• *Lavandula* (some)
• *Mahonia*
• *Olearia* (some)
• *Philadelphus* • *Pieris*
• *Pyracantha*
• *Viburnum*
• *Weigela*

HARDWOOD CUTTINGS

How long before roots form? After the cuttings have been inserted in a nursery bed in autumn, they will take up to a year to develop roots. The following autumn, carefully dig them up and plant them in a nursery bed until large enough for a border.

1 In autumn, when plants are dormant and leafless, take hardwood cuttings from mature shoots of the current season's growth. Cuttings should be 23–38 cm (9–15 in) long and will take up to a year to form roots.

2 Remove the lower leaves and trim the cutting's base just below a leaf-joint. Most plants increased by hardwood cuttings are deciduous, but some, like Ligustrum (Privet), are evergreen, partially evergreen or deciduous, depending on the local weather.

3 Use a spade to form a V-shaped trench, with one vertical side. Sprinkle sharp sand in the base and insert each cutting – a half to two-thirds of its length deep and about 10 cm (4 in) apart. Replace and firm the soil.

Shrubs to increase in this way
• *Buddleja* spp.
• *Cornus alba*
• *Cornus sericea* (syn. *Cornus stolonifera*)
• *Deutzia*
• *Forsythia*
• *Ligustrum ovalifolium*
• *Philadelphus*
• *Ribes*
• *Rubus*
• *Salix*
• *Sambucus*
• *Spiraea*
• *Symphoricarpos*
• *Tamarix*
• *Viburnum* (deciduous types)
• *Weigela*

Root cuttings

In this method, a part of a root is severed from the parent plant and encouraged to form new roots. There are two types: thin roots that are placed flat on compost in seed-trays (flats), and thick ones that are inserted vertically into pots. They are usually taken when dormant, mainly in late autumn and early winter. You can increase many plants in this way, but not grafted or budded plants, because their rootstocks actually come from a different plant.

What are root cuttings?

VERTICAL ROOT CUTTINGS

With thick root cuttings, you do not have to dig up the whole plant. Rather, just expose a few roots from around the plant's edge.

1 *Expose the plant's roots and sever some of them with secateurs or a sharp knife. Replace and firm soil around the remaining roots. Wash soil from roots.*

2 *Cut the roots into pieces 6–7.5 cm (2½–3 in) long. Make a flat cut at the end that was nearest the plant's centre, and a slope at the other.*

3 *Insert them, slope-end downwards, in equal parts moist peat and sharp sand, with the top flush with the surface. Cover with a 12 mm (½ in) layer of sharp sand.*

Aftercare

Gently water the compost and place the pot in a cold frame. By spring, roots will have formed; transfer the cuttings to a nursery bed until autumn, when you can plant them in a border.

Plants to increase in this way

- Anchusa azurea
- Catananche caerulea (Cupid's Dart)
- Eryngium
- Papaver orientale (Oriental Poppy)
- Rhus typhina (Stag's Horn Sumach)
- Romneya coulteri (Californian Tree Poppy)
- Verbascum (Mullein)

HORIZONTAL ROOT CUTTINGS

With thin root cuttings, plants are usually dug up entirely, with all roots exposed. It is an ideal way to produce a large number of new plants.

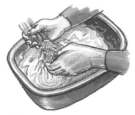  

1 *It is usual to dig up the entire plant, although roots can be exposed and removed. Wash them to remove all traces of soil. Select healthy roots.*

2 *Cut roots into pieces 6–7.5 cm (2½–3 in) long. Fill and firm a seed-tray (flat) with equal parts moist peat and sharp sand, with a dusting of sharp sand on top.*

3 *Space the cuttings on top and cover them with equal parts sharp sand and moist peat, leaving the surface about 12 mm (½ in) below the rim of the tray (flat).*

Aftercare

Gently water the compost and place the seed-tray (flat) in a cold frame. Regularly check that the compost is lightly moist, but it should not be saturated with water.

By the following spring, roots will have formed; either transfer the cuttings to individual pots or plant them in a nursery bed until the autumn, when you can plant them in a border.

Plants to increase in this way

- Phlox paniculata (Perennial Phlox)
- Primula denticulata (Drumstick Primula)

Leaf-bud cuttings

A leaf-bud cutting is a type of 'eye' cutting (see below), and this method is frequently used to increase camellias. Each leaf-bud cutting is formed from a half-ripened stem with a leaf attached, and a healthy bud in the joint between the stem and leaf. They are taken in summer, when the plant is actively growing. The leaf is essential to this type of cutting, as it provides a reserve of nourishment for the developing roots.

TAKING A LEAF-BUD CUTTING

Each cutting is prepared by cutting a sliver of wood from the stem, with the leaf and bud still attached. A sharp knife is essential for this task.

1 Cut a healthy stem from an established shrub. Then use a knife to cut a rounded section, containing the bud and leaf, from the stem.

2 Insert the half-moon-like sliver into a pot of equal parts moist peat and sharp sand until only the leaf shows above the compost.

3 After insertion, firm and water the compost; keep at 15–18°C (59–64°F). When shoots develop from the bud, you can pot up the cutting.

4 Transfer the rooted cutting to a small pot, using a lime-free potting compost. Place the young plant in a cold frame until it is well established.

Aftercare
Do not be tempted to plant young camellias in borders until they are firmly established; usually this is during the following spring. Provide shelter from cold winds and mix leafmould or peat into the soil. They need a position that is sheltered from early morning sun.

Plants to increase in this way
Usually confined to camellias, but occasionally also used for *Dracaena* and *Ficus elastica* (Rubber Plant).

EYE CUTTINGS

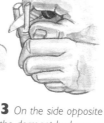

1 Used to increase grape vines, these cuttings are taken in autumn or winter, when the vine is dormant and free from leaves. Cut a healthy shoot from the vine.

2 Use sharp secateurs to cut the stem into 5 cm (2 in) long pieces, with a bud (eye) in the centre. Take care not to damage the dormant bud.

3 On the side opposite the dormant bud, use a sharp knife to cut a sliver of wood along the entire length of the cutting to remove the bark.

4 Place the cutting (eye upwards) on equal parts moist peat and sharp sand in a pot, and use bent pieces of wire to secure it into the compost.

Aftercare
Water, and keep at 13–16°C (55–61°F). When roots have formed, transfer the cuttings into individual pots and place them in gentle warmth until they are well established.

Plants to increase in this way
Grape vines only.

Stem and leaf-petiole cuttings

Astem cutting resembles a stem-tip cutting (see page 20), but without the tip; it is formed of a piece of stem and a leaf. This method is ideal for increasing houseplants that have long stems, and it enables you to take many cuttings from a single stem, rather than just one as with stem-tip cuttings. A leaf-petiole cutting consists of a leaf-stalk (petiole) and a leaf, and is a good way of increasing *Saintpaulia ionantha* (African Violet).

How do these differ?

INCREASING INDOOR IVIES BY STEM CUTTINGS

Spring and early summer are the best times to increase indoor ivies by stem cuttings. Follow the steps shown below and, when shoots develop from the cuttings, remove the plastic bag. They can then be potted up: put one, three or five cuttings in each pot – a high number of cuttings in each pot creates a bushy plant more quickly.

STEM CUTTINGS

Plants to increase in this way

- *Hedera canariensis* 'Gloire de Marengo' (Variegated Canary Island Ivy)
- *Hedera helix* (English Ivy) and encompassing a wide range of small-leaved ivies, including 'Anna Marie', 'Eva', 'Glacier', 'Goldchild', 'Jubilee', 'Kolibri' and 'Little Diamond'
- *Senecio macroglossus* 'Variegatus' (Cape Ivy, Wax Ivy)

1 *Use a sharp knife to cut a shoot into several cuttings. Cut slightly above each leaf-joint, but leave a stem about 3.5 cm (1½ in) below.*

2 *Fill a pot with equal parts moist peat and sharp sand and use a dibber (dibble) to form holes; put a cutting 18–30 mm (¾–1¼ in) deep in each one.*

3 *Firm the compost, water, and insert short, thin canes into the compost. Draw a plastic bag over the cuttings, and secure it with an elastic band around the pot.*

LEAF-PETIOLE CUTTINGS

1 *Water the parent plant the day before taking cuttings. Use a sharp knife to sever leaf-stalks close to their base.*

2 *Cut each leaf-stalk to about 3.5 cm (1½ in) long. Use a sharp knife so that cuttings are not left with ragged ends.*

3 *Fill and firm a pot with equal parts moist peat and sharp sand. Use a dibber to insert each stem 2.5 cm (1 in) deep. After inserting the cuttings in compost, cover with a plastic bag (see above). Remove the bag when shoots appear, and pot up the cuttings.*

Leaf cuttings

Are there many types?

Leaf cuttings range from whole leaves to cross-sections of leaves and both leaf-squares and leaf-triangles. Whole-leaf cuttings are laid flat on compost, and all the other types are inserted vertically into compost. You can increase many indoor and conservatory plants in temperate climates by means of leaf cuttings, and the particular method to select depends on the plant. A range of suitable plants for each type of leaf cutting is indicated below.

AFTER LEAF CUTTINGS DEVELOP ROOTS

As soon as small shoots appear from leaf-square and leaf-triangle cuttings, carefully transfer them to individual pots; place in gentle warmth until they are growing strongly. Leave the leaf-part still attached to the cutting; later, it will naturally wither and fall off. Strong sunlight and high temperatures must be avoided as they tend to 'fry' the thin leaves.

TAKING A LEAF-SQUARE CUTTING

1 Place a leaf on a flat board and cut along both sides of a main vein, so that the strip is about 30 mm (1¼ in) wide.

2 Cut each strip into squares, ensuring that each piece has several cut veins. Do not make the squares too small, as this increases the risk of cuttings decaying before they develop roots.

3 Use a knife to form slits in equal parts moist peat and sharp sand; insert cuttings 12 mm (½ in) deep, with the end nearest to the leaf-stalk facing downwards. Firm compost around them. Gently water the compost and place a transparent cover over the cuttings. Place in lightly shaded, gentle warmth.

4 When shoots and leaves develop from the cuttings, remove the cover and transfer the young plants into individual pots. Place in gentle warmth until established.

TAKING A LEAF-TRIANGLE CUTTING

1 The day before severing a healthy leaf, water the compost. Avoid leaving short spurs at the parent plant's base. If several leaves are removed, take them from different sides of the plant.

2 Turn the leaf upside-down on a flat board and use a sharp knife to cut off the stem, close to its base. Turn the leaf over so that its top side faces upwards.

3 Cut the leaf into triangles. The tip of the cutting should be towards the centre of the leaf, from where the stem originates.

4 Fill and firm equal parts moist peat and sharp sand in a seed-tray (flat). Use the blade of a knife to form a slit to about half the depth of the cutting. Insert a cutting in it and firm compost around it. Gently water the compost and cover with a transparent lid. Place in lightly shaded, gentle warmth.

5 When shoots and leaves develop from the cuttings, remove the cover and transfer the young plants into individual pots. Place in gentle warmth until established.

Plants to increase in these ways • *Begonia masoniana* (Iron Cross Begonia) • *Begonia rex* (Rex Begonia)

TAKING A LEAF CROSS-SECTION CUTTING

1 *Select a healthy leaf. Cut it off at its base, and use a sharp knife to cut it into sections 5 cm (2 in) wide.*

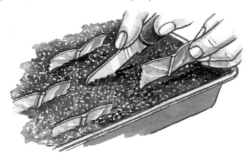

2 *Fill and firm equal parts moist peat and sharp sand in a seed-tray (flat). Form slits 18 mm (¾ in) deep; insert the bases of the cuttings in them. Firm compost around them, lightly water, cover with a plastic lid and place in gentle warmth.*

Plants to increase in this way
- *Sansevieria trifasciata* (Mother-in-law's Tongue) – see method shown below.
- *Sinningia speciosa* (Gloxinia)
- *Streptocarpus x hybridus* (Cape Primrose)

TAKING A WHOLE-LEAF CUTTING

1 *Select a healthy leaf from a well-watered plant and sever it at its base; do not leave short stubs.*

2 *Turn the leaf upside-down, sever the stem and cut across the veins, 18–25 mm (¾–1 in) apart. Do not cut through the leaf.*

3 *Place the leaf, cut side down, on compost in a seed-tray (flat). Insert U-shaped pieces of wire to hold it in place. Cover with a plastic lid and place in gentle warmth.*

4 *Regularly water the compost by standing the seed-tray in shallow water until moisture rises to the surface; when shoots appear, move young plants into individual pots.*

Plants to increase in this way
- *Begonia masoniana* (Iron Cross Begonia)
- *Begonia rex* (Rex Begonia)

INCREASING MOTHER-IN-LAW'S TONGUE

1 *The species* Sansevieria trifasciata *can be increased by cutting leaves into sections, but the variegated form needs to be increased by division (see page 31). Cut a healthy stem from a parent plant.*

2 *Use a sharp knife to cut a leaf into sections 5 cm (2 in) wide. Ensure that they are not turned upside-down as the sides towards the bottom of the leaf are the ones to be inserted in compost.*

3 *Fill and firm a shallow pot with equal parts moist peat and sharp sand. Use a knife to form a slit 18 mm (¾ in) deep and push cuttings into them. Firm the compost, lightly water and place in gentle warmth.*

Cane cuttings

Cane cuttings are frequently used to increase thick-stemmed houseplants, such as *Cordyline*, *Dieffenbachia*, *Dracaena* and *Yucca*, especially if they have lost their lower leaves and appear unsightly. The stems are cut into pieces, about 7.5 cm (3 in) long, and these are either laid flat on compost or inserted vertically into it. It is also possible to encourage stem cuttings of *Cordyline fruticosa* (Ti-palm), known as 'Ti-log' cuttings, to develop roots by placing them in water.

What are cane cuttings?

ROOTING TI-LOG CUTTINGS IN WATER

Cordyline fruticosa (Ti-palm) can be raised from Ti-log cuttings inserted vertically in water. Stand a cutting in a jar with 2.5 cm (1 in) of water in its base. Keep at 8°C (46°F); change the water every 4–5 days. After about four weeks, dormant buds start to grow and roots form; you can then transfer the cutting to loam-based compost in an individual pot.

VERTICAL TI-LOG CUTTINGS

1 Cut away a fraction of the lower end. Bought Ti-log cuttings often have had their ends coated in wax to reduce moisture loss.

2 Insert the cutting, cut end downwards and to about half its length, in equal parts moist peat and sharp sand in a pot. Firm the compost.

3 Water the compost and place the pot in an opaque bag in gentle warmth. Keep the compost moist and when shoots appear transfer to a larger pot.

Plants to increase in this way
Cordylines are frequently raised as Ti-log cuttings severed from plants growing in homes. However, many people return from holidays abroad with specially prepared Ti-log cuttings. Some are sold as 'Lucky Plants', with their ends coated in wax to prevent desiccation.

HORIZONTAL CANE CUTTINGS

1 Sever a shoot from a mother plant and cut into 6.5–7.5 cm (2¾–3 in) long pieces. Each piece must have at least one strong and healthy bud.

2 Fill and firm a pot with compost. Press each cutting, bud facing upwards, to half its thickness, and secure with bent pieces of wire.

3 Lightly water and cover with a plastic dome. Alternatively, insert short split canes in the compost and draw a plastic bag over the top. Seal around the pot with an elastic band.

Plants to increase in this way
- *Cordyline* spp.
- *Dieffenbachia* (Dumb Cane)
- *Dracaena*

Cacti and other succulents

Cacti and succulents are often grouped together, but botanically they are different. Cacti belong to the Cactaceae family, and are characterized by having areoles (resembling small pincushions) from which short hooks, spines or woolly hairs develop. With the exception of *Pereskia* and young *Opuntia* plants, cacti do not have normal leaves. Non-cactus succulents have fleshy leaves; there is a wide range of these plants, including many popular houseplants.

Are these the same?

SEEDS OR CUTTINGS?

As well as growing them from seeds, you can increase both cacti and other succulents through cuttings. These can be taken throughout the year, although spring and early summer are the best times. Moisture-retentive, well-aerated compost is essential, and a mixture of equal parts moist peat and sharp sand is suitable. Sprinkle sharp sand on the compost's surface as well. After inserting the cuttings, place the pot in gentle warmth and light shade.

STEM CUTTINGS

1 *Use a sharp knife to sever healthy stems from around the parent plant. Do not take them from just one position.*

2 *Use a dibber (dibble) to make a hole in lightly firmed compost and insert a cutting. Firm the compost, then lightly water.*

Prickly subjects

When holding prickly cacti, wear a pair of thin gardening gloves or rubber domestic ones. Alternatively, fold a piece of newspaper several times to form a 2.5 cm (1 in) wide band that can be wrapped around a prickly stem.

SUCCULENT LEAVES

1 *Gently pull off mature, fleshy leaves close to the stem. Do not leave short spurs, as it spoils the parent plant's shape.*

2 *Use a dibber (dibble) to form a wide slit into which a cutting can be inserted. You can put several cuttings in the same pot.*

Small and circular succulent leaves

You can encourage small, relatively flat, succulent leaves to form roots by pressing them into the surface of a mixture of equal parts sharp sand and moist peat. Succulents to increase in this way include *Sedum sieboldii* and its variegated form 'Mediovariegatum'.

3 *Firm compost around each cutting, then thoroughly but lightly water them. Place them in light shade and provide gentle warmth.*

4 *When young shoots develop from the cutting's base, transfer each cutting into an individual pot.*

Dividing herbaceous perennials

Is this method easy?

This is one of the simplest ways to increase herbaceous perennials, and the technique needs little equipment other than a couple of garden forks. Herbaceous perennials survive in cold regions because, during the cold winter months, they die down, leaving only old, dead stems showing above ground; each spring, they develop fresh shoots. In late autumn or early winter, this growth dies down and the plants survive by means of their dormant roots.

AUTUMN OR SPRING?

You can lift and divide herbaceous plants at any time between early autumn and mid-spring, whenever the soil and weather are suitable. Usually, this means autumn in areas where the weather is mild; but spring is better in areas where cold winters are regularly experienced.

Sometimes gardeners leave the old stems and do not cut them down until early spring, so that during winter they can protect the roots from severe frost. Old stems, leaves and flowerheads covered in frost also create an attractive winter feature, especially when caught by low rays from the sun.

DIVIDING A HERBACEOUS PERENNIAL

1 Use sharp secateurs to cut away any old stems still remaining on the plant, especially when dividing a clump in late winter or early spring.

2 Use a garden fork to lift the clump. Then, insert two garden forks, back to back, into the clump and draw the handles together to lever it apart.

3 Use your hands, if necessary, to finish pulling the clump apart. Do not create very small pieces, as they will not produce dominant plants.

4 Plant the divided pieces into borders. Use a trowel to form holes and draw friable soil around the roots. Firm the soil and water the entire area.

TYPES OF HERBACEOUS PERENNIAL

The root type of individual herbaceous perennials influences the way in which you should increase them. There are three different basic types of roots:

Fibrous roots: The majority of herbaceous perennials have spreading and fibrous roots; you can lift and divide these in the way shown on the left. They include:
• *Achillea* spp. • *Anaphalis* spp. • *Artemisia* spp. (herbaceous types) • *Aster* spp. (both summer- and autumn-flowering Michaelmas Daisies) • *Astilbe* spp. • *Astrantia* spp. • *Campanula* spp. (herbaceous types) • *Coreopsis* spp. (herbaceous types) • *Filipendula* spp. • *Geranium* spp. (not to be confused with pelargoniums) • *Helenium* spp. (herbaceous types) • *Helianthus* spp. (herbaceous types) • *Leucanthemum maximum* (syn. *Chrysanthemum maximum*; Shasta Daisy) • *Lysimachia* spp. (herbaceous types) • *Lythrum* spp. (herbaceous types) • *Monarda didyma* • *Phlox* spp. (herbaceous types) • *Rudbeckia* spp. (herbaceous types) • *Solidago* spp.

Fleshy roots: A few herbaceous perennials have woody, fleshy roots; lift the plant and use a sharp knife to separate crowns into several pieces. They include:
• *Delphinium* spp. • *Lupinus polyphyllus* (also increased from seeds and cuttings)

Rhizomatous roots: These are frequently grown in herbaceous borders; lift and divide the roots, and replant the divisions. They include *Iris germanica* (see page 32).

Dividing houseplants

This is the easiest way to increase, and revitalize, any fibrous-rooted houseplants that have become congested, their pots packed with roots, and that are producing little fresh growth. These have usually developed from a plant originally planted in the centre of a pot. Therefore, when dividing the plant, select young pieces from around the outside; often, the centre part is old and unproductive, and is best discarded. The new plants will be fresh and vigorous.

Why is it necessary?

OPTIMUM TIME

Houseplants that are mainly grown for their beautiful leaves are best divided in spring. Flowering houseplants, however, should be divided after their flowers fade – the earlier the better. Leave those houseplants that flower in autumn until spring before dividing them.

Dividing houseplants in spring (or as early as possible) gives young plants a chance to become fully established in summer, while growing strongly.

Before the newly divided parts are fully established, place them in gentle warmth and light shade.

DIVIDING A PEACE LILY

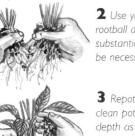

1 To check if a clump-forming houseplant needs repotting, remove the pot. A mat of roots indicates that division is needed.

2 Use your fingers to pull the rootball apart into several substantially sized pieces. It may be necessary to cut some roots.

3 Repot each new plant into a clean pot; position at the same depth as before, then trickle and firm compost around the roots. Then, water the plant.

DIVIDING A MOTHER-IN-LAW'S TONGUE

1 The yellow-edged form Sansevieria trifasciata var. laurentii is best increased by division. Pull the rootball apart into several pieces.

2 Add potting compost to a pot and put a new plant in place. Adjust the compost's height, so the plant is at the same depth as before.

3 Hold a plant and trickle and firm compost around its roots. Leave a 12 mm (½ in) gap between the compost and the pot's rim. Then water the plant.

DIVIDING A SAINTPAULIA

Saintpaulia ionantha (African Violet) can be increased from leaf-petiole cuttings (see page 25), as well as by severing a healthy leaf and suspending the leaf-stalk in clean water (see page 21), but congested plants can also be divided. In spring or early summer, remove a congested plant from its pot and gently tease it into separate pieces. Ensure that each new plant is a respectable size. Then repot them into individual pots. Firm the compost and water.

SUITABLE HOUSEPLANTS FOR DIVISION

Many houseplants are good candidates for division, including the following:
- *Aspidistra elatior* (Cast Iron Plant)
- *Calathea* spp.
- *Carex* spp.
- *Ctenanthe oppenheimiana* 'Tricolor' (Never Never Plant)
- Ferns (many clustered types are suitable)
- *Maranta* spp. (many are suitable)
- *Saintpaulia ionantha* (African Violet)
- *Spathiphyllum wallisii* (Peace Lily)
- *Stenotaphrum secundatum* (Buffalo Grass)
- *Stenotaphrum secundatum* 'Variegatum' (Variegated Buffalo Grass)

Bulbs, corms, tubers and rhizomes

Are they the same?

Bulbs, corms, tubers and rhizomes are all powerhouses of stored energy (see below for an explanation of what each one is). They are underground or partly underground and, given the right conditions, will create spectacular and assured displays of flowers. Daffodils, for example, are famed for their spring flowers. Because of their different structures, the methods of increasing them markedly differ. However, with all of them, only propagate from healthy plants.

WHAT ARE THEY?

- **Bulbs:** fleshy, overlapping modified leaves attached to a basal plate and enclosing a young shoot (daffodils, hyacinths and onions).
- **Corms:** thickened stem bases, usually covered with a papery skin (crocus and gladiolus).
- **Rhizomes:** underground or partly buried, horizontal stems. Some are slender, such as *Convallaria majalis* (Solomon's Seal); *Iris germanica* (Flag Iris) has partly buried, thick, corrugated rhizomes.
- **Tubers:** thickened and swollen stems or roots. Dahlias are root tubers; potatoes are stem tubers.

DIVIDING DAHLIA TUBERS

In autumn, about a week after their foliage has been blackened by frost, use a garden fork to lift tubers from borders where they have been growing. Cut stems to 15 cm (6 in) high and position upside down for a couple of weeks in an airy shed. Then place in boxes of slightly damp peat.

In early to mid-spring, use a sharp knife to divide clumps of tubers; each new plant must contain a stem (which contains growth buds).

Alternatively, where there are only few stems, cut these in half vertically. Each part of the stem must have at least one healthy growth bud.

Dust cut surfaces with a fungicide, then plant individual pieces directly into a border, in holes 15 cm (6 in) deep. Before you plant, insert a cane to mark the position of the tuber.

DIVIDING RHIZOMATOUS IRISES

Lifting and dividing rhizomes of *Iris germanica* (Flag Iris) as soon as its flowers fade will ensure that flower quality does not diminish. Alternatively, lift and divide the rhizomes in late summer.

Carefully dig up the entire plant and use a sharp knife to divide clumps, selecting young pieces from around the outside. Discard old, central parts.

Each piece must have one or two fans of leaves. Trim off the top third of foliage.

Replant the young plants, either in a nursery bed or in a border, to the same depth as before.

Bulbs

Bulbils develop around the parent bulbs. After the plant has flowered and when the foliage has died down naturally, lift the bulbs and carefully remove the bulbils. In late summer or early autumn, large bulbils can be replanted.

Small bulbils take about two seasons before they are large enough to produce flowers. In autumn, form a flat-based drill, 5–7.5 cm (2–3 in) deep, with sharp sand in its base. Space out the bulbils and cover them with friable soil. After a couple of years, lift and plant them in their flowering positions.

Corms

Towards autumn, old corms shrivel, leaving a new one that will flower during the following year. Additionally, cormlets cluster around its base. In autumn, carefully fork up plants and cut each stem 12 mm (½ in) above the corm. Discard the old, shrivelled corm and in winter store the new one in a dry, vermin-proof shed.

Remove the cormlets; place in a dry shed during winter. In early spring, form a drill 5 cm (2 in) deep and line it with sharp sand; space out the cormlets and cover them with friable soil. Lift them in autumn and store in winter. Repeat this during the following year before they reach flowering size.

Layering shrubs, trees and climbers

This is both an easy and an assured way to increase shrubs, trees and climbers. However, it is not quick and may take up to a year before the layer develops roots and can be severed from the parent plant. It is then planted either into a nursery bed or directly into a border. For shrubs and trees to be layered, it is essential that a relatively young shoot is low enough to be lowered to the soil, and sufficiently pliable to be bent into position with its tip upright.

Is layering difficult?

PREPARING THE GROUND

Layering is an excellent way for home gardeners to increase shrubs and climbers, but the area where the stem is layered must be left undisturbed for up to a year. Therefore, before starting to layer a plant, remove all weeds from the area, especially perennial types that will regularly produce new shoots unless their roots are dug up.

LAYERING A SHRUB

1 *Select a healthy, low-growing, vigorous shoot that is up to two years old. Form a shallow trench that slopes to 7.5–15 cm (3–6 in) deep at its lowest point, 23–45 cm (9–18 in) from the shoot's tip. Lower the shoot into the depression and bend its tip upright. Wound the stem, either by making a tongued cut at the point of the bend or by cutting halfway around the stem and removing the bark.*

2 *Use a piece of bent wire or a wooden peg to hold the stem in the ground. Firm soil over the stem, so that its surface is level. Insert a bamboo cane and tie the shoot to it, to hold it secure and upright.*

3 *When new growth appears on the layered shoot, remove the soil, sever the shoot from the parent and plant into a nursery bed or directly into a border.*

Twenty shrubs, trees and climbers that can be layered

For further information about these plants, refer to the A–Z of propagating plants (see pages 42–78).
• *Amelanchier* (June Berry/Snowy Mespilus)
• *Azalea* • *Chaenomeles* (Japanese Quince/Cydonia/Japonica) • *Chimonanthus praecox* (Winter Sweet) • *Clematis* • *Cornus alba* (Red-barked Dogwood) • *Cotoneaster* • *Forsythia* (Golden Bells) • *Garrya elliptica* • *Hamamelis* (Witch Hazel) • *Jasminum nudiflorum* (Winter-flowering Jasmine) • *Liriodendron tulipifera* (Tulip Tree) • *Magnolia* • *Parthenocissus* • *Pieris* • *Piptanthus* • *Rhododendron* • *Rhus typhina* (Stag's Horn Sumach) • *Viburnum* • *Wisteria*

TIP-LAYERING

This is a popular and easy way to increase plants with long, pendulous stems that can have their tips lowered to the ground and buried in soil. Popular plants that can be tip-layered include Blackberries, Loganberries and other Hybrid Berries.

1 *During late summer or early autumn, select a long, young, healthy stem and lower it to the ground. Use a trowel to form a hole, 7.5–15 cm (3–6 in) deep, where the tip touches the ground. Alternatively, to make transplanting easier when roots have formed, bury the tip in a 15 cm (6 in) wide pot that is itself sunk to its rim in the soil to help keep the compost moist and cool.*

2 *Position the tip in the hole and use a piece of bent wire to hold it in position. Cover the tip with soil and level and firm the surface. Then, water the area, keeping it moist until rooting is complete. Rooting takes a few months; in spring (sometimes earlier) sever the stem about 30 cm (1 ft) from the tip. The rooted tip can then be transplanted to a nursery bed or, preferably, its final growing position.*

Layering houseplants

Is this method quick?

Layering is an easy and assured way to increase houseplants. However, it is not fast; it often takes several weeks for new roots to form, when the rooted parts can be severed from the parent plant and transferred to individual pots. It is well suited to increasing houseplants with long and flexible stems (see below for a range of suitable plants) and it has the advantage of a high success rate. It is also a technique that inevitably captures the attention of children.

GETTING THE TIMING RIGHT

Late spring and early summer are the best times to layer houseplants, when they are starting to grow strongly after, perhaps, a partially dormant period during winter. This subsequently allows plenty of time for the layered stems to develop roots, and for you to sever and transfer them to pots before the arrival of the less vigorous growing days of autumn. Always check that the parent plant and the shoots being layered are healthy and free from pests and diseases.

LAYERING A HEDERA (IVY)

1 Select a healthy shoot and bend it sharply, without severing it, 10–15 cm (4–6 in) from its tip.

2 Press the bend into a pot of compost and secure it in place with a bent wire; firm the compost, and water.

3 Keep the compost moist and, when roots have formed, use sharp scissors to sever the stem close to the new plant.

LAYERING A PHILODENDRON SCANDENS (SWEETHEART PLANT)

1 Lower a stem into a pot of compost and press it into the surface; secure it with bent wire.

2 Firm the compost around the young shoot; water the compost to settle it around the shoot.

3 When young shoots appear from the layer's tip, use sharp scissors to sever it from the parent.

HOUSEPLANTS FOR LAYERING

- *Cissus antarctica* (Kangaroo Vine)
- *Cissus rhombifolia* (Grape Ivy)
- *Epipremnum aureum* (Devil's Ivy)
- *Hedera canariensis* (Canary Island Ivy) and cultivars
- *Hedera helix* (many variegated forms)
- *Philodendron scandens* (Sweetheart Plant)
- *Plectranthus coleoides* 'Marginatus' (Swedish Ivy)

Putting pots in the same tray

When several stems are layered at the same time from a parent plant, place all the pots in a large plastic tray. This makes it easier to move the parent plant and, perhaps, three or more small pots at once without disturbing the layered shoots.

Air-layering houseplants

Air-layering a houseplant is a fascinating way to give houseplants such as the popular *Ficus elastica* (Rubber Plant) a fresh lease of life if it has become bare of leaves around the lower part of its main stem. However, there should be about 45 cm (18 in) of stem at the top that is packed with healthy leaves. Although air-layering can be performed throughout the year, it is most successful when carried out from spring to late summer.

What does this method involve?

LONG-LIFE PROBLEM

A few indoor foliage plants have such a long life expectancy and tree-like form that their stems often become unsightly when bare of leaves. The initial reaction is to throw them away. However, you can air-layer them and encourage them to be attractive plants again – below is a step-by-step sequence explaining how to achieve this.

AIR-LAYERING A RUBBER PLANT

1 Use a sharp knife to make an upward-slanting cut, two-thirds through the stem and 7.5–10 cm (3–4 in) below the lowest leaf.

2 Use a matchstick to keep the cut open; dust the surfaces with hormone rooting powder. Cut off the ends of long matchsticks.

3 Loosely wind a 20–25 cm (8–10 in) wide strip of clear polythene around the cut; tie below and fill with moist peat. Seal the top.

4 Keep the parent plant's compost moist. About six weeks later, roots will appear inside the polythene. Sever the stem and remove the polythene.

5 Before roots become dry, pot up the plant into potting compost. Until it is established, support the plant with a cane.

OTHER HOUSEPLANTS TO AIR-LAYER

Ficus elastica (Rubber Plant), and its forms, is the most popular houseplant for air-layering, but there are two others that will also respond to this treatment:
- *Dieffenbachia maculata* (Dumb Cane)
- *Monstera deliciosa* (Swiss Cheese Plant)

THE OLD PLANT

Do not throw away the old plant, as it can be encouraged to develop into another plant for the home. The old plant will still be growing in its pot; cut back the stem to just above a bud and place in gentle warmth. Keep the compost moist, and within a few weeks young shoots will appear.

AIR-LAYERING OUTDOORS

Also known as 'marcottage' and 'gootee' layering, this form of encouraging stems to develop roots while still attached to a parent plant was practised in India and China from early times. It was used on trees that were too difficult to raise from cuttings, or had stems that could not be lowered to the ground and partly buried until rooted.

'Marcottage' or 'gootee' layering involved cutting a stem just under a leaf-bud with an upward-sloping cut, and using a small stick to wedge it open. Around it was packed a ball of sticky soil, held in place with coir fibre. Because this method of layering was used before polythene was available, to retain moisture around the cut stem a small bamboo bucket was suspended above and a wick used to transfer moisture to it. This was undertaken in the 'wet season', just when the tree started active growth. In 3–4 months, roots formed and the shoot was cut from the parent and potted up or planted out.

Runners and plantlets

Are these easy to root?

The pegging of runners into compost and the rooting of plantlets to encourage the development of new plants both seem to fascinate people, especially children. They are ways to increase houseplants that can be performed indoors as well as in greenhouses and conservatories. It is even possible to ask any friends who have a **Mexican Hat Plant** or a **Chandelier Plant** (see below and right) for a few plantlets that you can take away and encourage to form roots.

BOTANICAL MAZE!

Both the Mexican Hat Plant and the Chandelier Plant have had radical name changes in recent years, and in older gardening books you might find different names from present-day ones. The Mexican Hat Plant (see below) is now called *Kalanchoe daigremontiana*, but in earlier years was known as *Bryophyllum daigremontianum*; the Chandelier Plant (see opposite page) is now known as *Kalanchoe delagoensis*, earlier as *Kalanchoe tubiflora* and *Bryophyllum tubiflorum*.

SPIDER PLANT

1 *Spider Plants have long, trailing, arching stems with small plantlets at their ends that can be encouraged to form roots.*

2 *Without severing the stem, use a piece of bent wire to secure a plantlet into a small pot of compost. Water, and place the pot in gentle warmth.*

3 *When the plantlet develops shoots and roots, sever the stem close to the plant (also next to the parent plant).*

For easy moving ...

Usually, several plantlets are inserted in pots at the same time. To enable the parent plant and pots of pegged-down plantlets to be easily moved together as a unit, without too much disturbance, place them all on a large, flat, plastic tray.

MEXICAN HAT PLANT

1 *Hat-like, succulent leaves develop plantlets along their edges that can be detached and encouraged to form roots.*

2 *Either scatter the plantlets on compost in pots, or space them out and, with a small dibber (dibble), insert them into the compost.*

3 *Press the plantlets into the compost, keep lightly moist and place in gentle warmth. When roots form, carefully lift out the plantlets.*

4 *When growing strongly, transfer each plantlet to a separate pot. Lightly water and place in gentle warmth until well established.*

KALANCHOE DELAGOENSIS (CHANDELIER PLANT)

Carefully detach
and save plantlets

Space out the
plantlets, so that
they do not
touch each other

1 *With age, plantlets at the ends of the succulent, tubular leaves develop hair-like roots. You can detach the plantlets and encourage them to grow into individual plants.*

2 *Gently pull off the plantlets and space them out on the surface of moisture-retentive compost. Use the point of a knife or pencil to space them out.*

Gently press
plantlets into
the compost

Water from below to avoid
disturbing the plantlets

3 *Individually, gently press the plantlets into the compost. Unless their roots are in close contact with the compost, development will be retarded.*

4 *Do not water the plantlets from above. Instead, stand the pots in a bowl shallowly filled with water. When moisture rises to the surface, remove the pots and allow them to drain.*

Carefully firm
compost around
the roots

5 *When the plantlets have developed roots and started to grow, transfer them either singly into small pots, or as clusters of three into a large pot to create a more dominant feature.*

OTHER PLANTS TO INCREASE FROM PLANTLETS AND BULBILS

- *Asplenium bulbiferum* (Hen-and-chicken Fern, Mother Fern): an indoor and greenhouse plant with mid-green fronds on which bulbils (small, immature bulbs) grow. These can be detached and pressed into compost in pots.
- *Tolmiea menziesii* (Pig-a-back Plant, Youth-on-age): hardy evergreen perennial, grown indoors as well as in gardens. Plantlets develop on the leaves; you can detach and root these.

Increasing roses

In budding, a healthy bud from a desired variety is united with a rootstock of another variety of known vigour and suitability for a specific type of soil. This is the main method of increasing Hybrid Teas (large-flowered bush roses) and Floribundas (cluster-flowered bush roses); you can also use it to create half-, full and weeping standard roses. Taking cuttings is an alternative, but it is best suited to vigorous Floribundas, most shrub roses, ramblers and vigorous climbers.

BUDDING STANDARD ROSES

The technique of making T-shaped cuts and inserting buds is exactly the same for budding standard roses as for bush types. The difference is that three buds are used and inserted well above ground level – 75–90 cm (2½–3 ft) for half-standards, and 1.2–1.3 m (4–4½ ft) for full standards. Prepare rootstocks by allowing, and supporting, a single stem to grow to well above the desired budding height. Success in budding roses depends on tackling it at the right time of year, when the rind lifts easily from the wood – usually about mid-summer, but possibly earlier in mild districts.

BUDDING BUSH ROSES

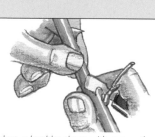

1 *Select a healthy shoot, with a growth bud, of the chosen variety (it is usual to cut this earlier and keep it damp by wrapping it in moist sacking). Cut off the leaves, leaving leaf-stalks 12 mm (½ in) long. Insert a sharp knife 18 mm (¾ in) above the bud and, passing under it, emerge 12 mm (½ in) below it, so the bud is cut off with a sliver of wood attached.*

2 *When budding Hybrid Tea or Floribunda roses, scrape and wipe away loose soil from around the base of the rootstock, 3.5–5 cm (1½–2 in) above the ground. Then make a T-shaped cut, with the vertical cut about 3.5 cm (1½ in) long and the horizontal one 12–18 mm (½–¾ in) wide. Use the spatula end of a budding knife to lift the rind.*

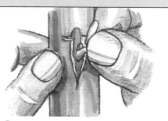

3 *Hold the bud by its leaf-stalk and remove the sliver of wood behind it. Then, from the top end, carefully slide it into the T-shaped cut. It may be necessary again to use the spatula end of a budding knife to open the flaps more fully. When the bud is secure in the T-cut, use a sharp knife to cut off any woody part that may protrude above it.*

4 *Secure the bud firmly in position with either raffia or a proprietary, thin, elastic-type budding tie. When using raffia, first make it more pliable by immersing it in water for a few minutes. Wrap raffia around the top and bottom of the bud, without covering it. Ensure that the leaf-stalk is not knocked or damaged.*

5 *Three to four weeks later, a successful uniting of the bud with the rootstock is indicated by a plump bud; at the same time the leaf-stalk drops off. At this stage, use a sharp knife to cut the raffia on the side opposite the bud. If left, the raffia (or proprietary budding tie) would constrict the flow or sap and prevent growth.*

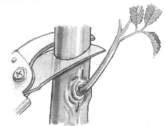

6 *Keep the area free from weeds and, in early or mid-spring of the following year, use sharp secateurs to cut off the top growth, about 12 mm (½ in) above the bud. Take care not to knock or damage the bud and its developing shoot. Also pull off (close to their bases) sucker-like shoots growing from the rootstock.*

Whip-and-tongue and saddle grafting

Whip-and-tongue grafting is a type of graft widely used to create new apple and pear trees; it gains its name from the tongue-like lips that help to hold the varietal part (scion) to the rooted part (rootstock). It should be tackled at the end of the dormant season, in early spring just as trees are breaking into growth. Saddle grafting is suitable for rhododendrons and is usually performed in a greenhouse in late winter or early spring.

What do these methods entail?

WHIP-AND-TONGUE GRAFTING

1 *The varietal part (scion) is formed of a healthy one-year-old shoot with 3–4 healthy buds. Cut the top slightly above a bud; the lower cut should form a slant 3.5 cm (1½ in) long and opposite the lowest bud. Halfway along this slant, make an upward cut to form a tongue.*

2 *Cut the root part (rootstock) 7.5–10 cm (3–4 in) above the ground and make a 3.5 cm (1½ in) long slanting cut at its top. Halfway along this slant make a down-ward cut to form a tongue; this will later enable it to unite with the scion and to hold it in place before raffia is wrapped around it.*

3 *Position the scion on top of the stock and push the 'tongues' together, so that the edges of both the stock and scion join each other. Then, bind raffia around the graft and cover with grafting wax. Also put a small blob of wax on top of the scion to seal its top.*

SADDLE GRAFTING RHODODENDRONS

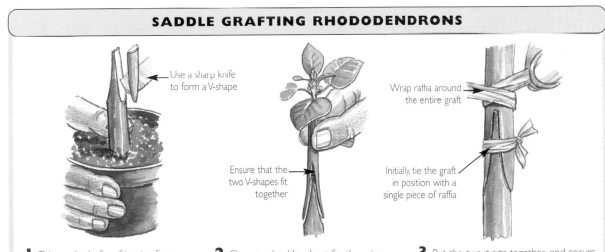

Use a sharp knife to form a V-shape

Ensure that the two V-shapes fit together

Wrap raffia around the entire graft

Initially, tie the graft in position with a single piece of raffia

1 *This method of grafting is often used to propagate named varieties of rhododendrons and is usually performed in gentle warmth in a greenhouse in late winter or early spring. Cut the rootstock 5–7.5 cm (2–3 in) high and form an inverted V-shape (as illustrated).*

2 *Choose a healthy shoot for the scion, about 7.5–10 cm (3–4 in) long and with a healthy terminal bud. Preferably, its thickness should be about the same as the rootstock. Cut a V-shaped piece out of its base, so that it will closely fit the stock.*

3 *Put the two parts together, and secure with a piece of raffia to initially hold them together. Then securely wrap raffia around them. It is not necessary to cover the raffia with wax, as the plant remains in a greenhouse and moisture can be kept off the grafted area.*

Grafting to rejuvenate fruit trees

When is this necessary?

In earlier years, before the introduction of the range of dwarfing rootstocks we have today for apples and pears, many trees eventually grew too large, sometimes 6 m (20 ft) or more high. This meant that looking after the tree, as well as picking the crop, was difficult. Apart from slowing the growth of apple and pear trees by cutting back their roots, another solution was rejuvenating the tree by grafting new varieties onto the branches.

TOPWORKING AND FRAMEWORK GRAFTING

These are two different ways of changing the nature of a fruit tree and introducing different varieties.
- Topworking involves radically cutting off the main limbs and creating a completely new branch system (see below).

- Framework grafting is less drastic and, initially, entails leaving branches intact and grafting many scions onto a tree, using a wide range of grafts (see the opposite page for the ones that are most widely used).

TOPWORKING

Crown grafting, also known as rind grafting, is the main form of topworking, and initially involves cutting all main branches to 60–90 cm (2–3 ft) from the tree's 'crotch'. The stubs of the branches that remain should not be more than 13 cm (5 in) wide, and preferably only 7.5–10 cm (3–4 in). Sometimes, branches are cut off to about 1.2 m (4 ft) from the crotch in autumn or winter, and then recut in late winter or early spring to produce freshly cut surfaces; use a sharp knife to pare the surfaces smooth.

1 *Use a sharp knife to make one, two or three vertical cuts, 3.5 cm (1½ in) long, down the side of each stub.*

2 *With a knife, gently prise open the upper edges of each cut and insert a scion (see below for preparation and insertion).*

PREPARING THE SCIONS

- Form scions from one-year-old shoots; cut these off in winter, label them and 'heel' them in a shaded nursery bed.

- When grafting time arrives (mid- to late spring for topworking), wash them to remove soil.

- Each shoot provides several scions, each formed of 3–4 buds, but these should not be taken from the soft top of the shoot.

- Prepare each scion by cutting just above a bud at the top, and just above the fourth or fifth bud at the base. Then, make a sloping cut about 3.5 cm (1½ in) long on the side opposite the lowest bud.

- To enable the scion to fit the cut more easily, trim 6 mm (¼ in) off the base, cutting diagonally on the bud side.

- Gently insert the scion into the cut, until about 3.5 cm (1½ in) deep.

- Continue with step 3 (illustrated right).

3 *When the scions are in place, wrap soft string around each stub, to the depth of the original cuts.*

4 *Use a brush to cover the string, cuts, tops of the pared stubs and tips of the scions with grafting wax.*

FRAMEWORK GRAFTING

Stub grafting

1 *This graft uses tension to hold a scion in place. From above, cut two-thirds of the way through a major shoot, close to where it joins a branch. The shoot's weight pulls the cut open and enables you to insert a scion that is 7–8 buds long and has a tapering, V-shaped base.*

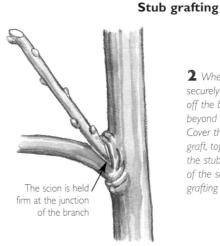

The scion is held firm at the junction of the branch

2 *When the scion is securely in place, cut off the branch, slightly beyond the graft. Cover the base of the graft, together with the stub and the tops of the scions, in grafting wax.*

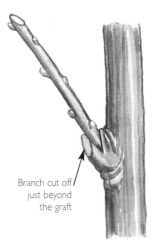

Branch cut off just beyond the graft

Inverted-L graft

You can use an inverted-L graft, together with side grafts, to create sideshoots. Make an L-shaped cut, with sides 2.5–3 cm (1–1¼ in) long, in the side of a thick branch. The cut creates a flap, into which you can insert a scion that is 7–8 buds long and has a tapering base. When in place, with one of the edges of the scion next to the cut's edge, use a thin nail to hold it in place. Cover with grafting wax.

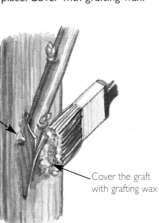

A nail holds the graft in position

Cover the graft with grafting wax

Side graft

Create sideshoots by inserting scions into downward cuts – 2.5–3 cm (1–1¼ in) long and forming a stiff lip – made in a branch. Push a scion, 7–8 buds long and with a base cut to a slightly triangular shape, into the flap; one side must be aligned with the edge of the cut. Cover with grafting wax.

Suitable trees and timing

- Framework grafting, which is tackled when sap is starting to rise in spring, is suitable for apples and pears, as well as stone fruits such as plums and cherries.
- Topworking can also be used on these fruits, but in preparation for grafting do not cut back the branches of stone fruits when the trees are dormant in the winter, because fungal diseases such as silver leaf are likely to enter through cut surfaces.

Positioning framework grafts

Because framework grafts have a radical influence on the shape of the ensuing tree, it is essential to choose their positions with care. Spread them evenly around a tree, not crowded on one side. It is also worth remembering that vertical grafts form stronger shoots and branches than horizontal ones. For that reason, the scions are best positioned vertically.

Sap-drawers

When topwork grafting, leave in place a few main shoots that originate below the grafts to act as sap-drawers; you can later remove (or graft) them when the earlier grafts have developed strong shoots. Leaving shoots helps to feed the roots as well as encouraging growth. There is no need to consider sap-drawing shoots when framework grafting.

Common names index

The plants included here (pages 42–50) are listed by their common names, with cross-references to their botanical names, which are featured on pages 51–78. This ensures that you can easily find the information you need to increase a plant. Some common names refer to specific plants, and others to a group of plants (a genus). For example, African Violet refers to the species *Saintpaulia ionantha*, while Birch refers to *Betula*, the genus to which all species of birch belong.

A   A–Z OF COMMON NAMES   B

Aaron's Rod See *Verbascum thapsus*.

Adam's Needle See *Yucca filamentosa*.

African Daisy See *Arctotis* x *hybrida*.

African Lily See *Agapanthus*.

African Marigold See *Tagetes erecta*.

African Violet See *Saintpaulia ionantha*.

Almond See *Prunus*, Almonds.

Alpine Snow Gum See *Eucalyptus niphophila*.

Alpine Wallflower See *Erysimum alpinum*.

American Sweet Gum See *Liquidambar styraciflua*.

Angelica See *Angelica archangelica*.

Aniseed See *Pimpinella anisum*.

Annual Campion See *Lychnis viscaria*.

Annual Chrysanthemum See *Chrysanthemum carinatum*.

Annual Mallow See *Lavatera trimestris*.

Annual Phlox See *Phlox drummondii*.

Annual Woodruff See *Asperula orientalis*.

Apple See *Malus*.

Apple of Peru See *Nicandra physalodes*.

Apricot See *Prunus*, Apricots.

Arum Lily See *Zantedeschia aethiopica*.

Avens See *Geum*.

Azalea See *Rhododendron*.

Baby Blue Eyes See *Nemophila menziesii*.

Baby's Breath See *Gypsophila elegans* and *Gypsophila paniculata*.

Bachelor's Button See *Gomphrena globosa*.

Bachelor's Buttons See *Kerria japonica* 'Pleniflora'.

Bald Cypress See *Taxodium distichum*.

Balloon Flower See *Platycodon grandiflorus*.

Balm See *Melissa officinalis*.

Balsam See *Impatiens balsamina*.

Bamboos See Bamboo.

Barberry See *Berberis*.

Barberton Daisy See *Gerbera jamesonii*.

Barrenwort See *Epimedium*.

Basil (Sweet) See *Ocimum basilicum*.

Bay See *Laurus nobilis*.

Bay Laurel See *Laurus nobilis*.

Bear's Breeches See *Acanthus mollis* and *Acanthus spinosus*.

Beauty Bush See *Kolkwitzia amabilis*.

Bee Balm See *Monarda didyma*.

Beech See *Fagus sylvatica*.

Begonia Vine See *Cissus discolor*.

Belladonna Lily See *Amaryllis belladonna*.

Bellflowers See *Campanula*.

Bells of Ireland See *Molucella laevis*.

Birch See *Betula*.

Bird Cherry See *Prunus padus*.

Bishop's Hat See *Epimedium*.

Bistort See *Persicaria bistorta* 'Superba'.

Black-eyed Susan See *Rudbeckia hirta* and *Thunbergia alata*.

B | **A–Z OF COMMON NAMES** | **C**

Blackthorn See *Prunus spinosa*.

Blanket Flower See *Gaillardia aristata* and *Gaillardia pulchella*.

Blazing Star See *Liatris*.

Bleeding Heart See *Dicentra*.

Bluebeard See *Caryopteris* x *clandonensis*.

Bluebell See *Hyacinthoides hispanica*.

Blue Blossom See *Ceanothus thyrsiflorus*.

Blue Lace Flower See *Trachelium caeruleum*.

Blue Lungwort See *Pulmonaria officinalis*.

Blue Poppy See *Meconopsis betonicifolia*.

Borage See *Borago officinalis*.

Boston Ivy See *Parthenocissus tricuspidata*.

Bottle Brush See *Callistemon*.

Brandy Bottle See *Nuphar lutea*.

Bridal Wreath See *Spiraea* 'Arguta'.

Broom See *Cytisus* and *Genista*.

Buddleia See *Buddleja* spp.

Buffalo Grass See *Stenotaphrum secundatum*.

Bugbane See *Cimicifuga*.

Bugle See *Ajuga*.

Burning Bush See *Bassia scoparia* f. *trichophylla* and *Dictamnus albus*.

Busy Lizzie See *Impatiens walleriana*.

Butterfly Bush See *Buddleja davidii*.

Butterfly Flower See *Schizanthus pinnatus*.

Cabbage Gum See *Eucalyptus pauciflora*.

Calico Bush See *Kalmia latifolia*.

California Bluebell See *Phacelia campanularia*.

Californian Lilac See *Ceanothus*.

Californian Poppy See *Eschscholzia californica*.

Californian Tree Poppy See *Romneya coulteri*.

Calla Lily See *Zantedeschia aethiopica* 'Crowborough'.

Camass See *Camassia quamash*.

Canary Creeper See *Tropaeolum peregrinum*.

Candytuft See *Iberis umbellata*.

Canterbury Bell See *Campanula medium*.

Cape Asparagus See *Aponogeton distachyos*.

Cape Ivy See *Senecio macroglossus* 'Variegatus'.

Cape Pondweed See *Aponogeton distachyos*.

Cape Primrose See *Streptocarpus* x *hybridus*.

Caraway See *Carum carvi*.

Cast Iron Plant See *Aspidistra elatior*.

Catmint See *Nepeta* x *faassenii*.

Cedar See *Cedrus*.

Chandelier Plant See *Kalanchoe delagoensis*.

Checkerbloom See *Sidalcea malviflora*.

Cherry See *Prunus*, Cherries.

Cherry Laurel See *Prunus laurocerasus*.

Cherry Pie See *Heliotropium arborescens*.

Cherry Plum See *Prunus cerasifera*.

Chervil See *Anthriscus cerefolium*.

Chile Pine See *Araucaria araucana*.

Chilean Potato Tree See *Solanum crispum*.

China Aster See *Callistephus chinensis*.

Chinese Honeysuckle See *Lonicera nitida*.

Chinese Plumbago See *Ceratostigma willmottianum*.

Chinese Virginia Creeper See *Parthenocissus henryana*.

Chinese Windmill Palm See *Trachycarpus fortunei*.

Chinese Wisteria See *Wisteria sinensis*.

Chinese Woodbine See *Lonicera tragophylla*.

Chives See *Allium schoenoprasum*.

Christmas Rose See *Helleborus niger*.

Chusan Palm See *Trachycarpus fortunei*.

Clarkia See *Clarkia elegans* and *Clarkia pulchella*.

Clary See *Salvia sclarea*.

Clematis See *Clematis*.

Climbing Bittersweet See *Celastrus orbiculatus*.

Cockscomb See *Celosia argentea* var. *cristata*.

Coleus See *Solenostemon scutellarioides*.

Colewort See *Crambe cordifolia*.

Columbine See *Aquilegia vulgaris*.

Comfrey See *Symphytum grandiflorum*.

Common Box See *Buxus sempervirens*.

Common Daisy See *Bellis perennis*.

Common Evening Primrose See *Oenothera biennis*.

Common Flax See *Linum usitatissimum*.

Common Holly See *Ilex aquifolium*.

Common Hydrangea See *Hydrangea macrophylla*.

Common Laurel See *Prunus laurocerasus*.

Common Lilac See *Syringa vulgaris*.

Common Mullein See *Verbascum thapsus*.

Common Privet See *Ligustrum ovalifolium*.

Common Snowdrop See *Galanthus nivalis*.

Common Spindle Tree See *Euonymus europaeus*.

Common White Jasmine See *Jasminum officinale*.

Common Wormwood See *Artemisia absinthium*.

Coneflower See *Rudbeckia fulgida* and *Rudbeckia hirta*.

Coral Flower See *Heuchera sanguinea*.

Coriander See *Coriandrum sativum*.

Corn Cockle See *Agrostemma githago* 'Milas'.

Cornelian Cherry See *Cornus mas*.

Cornflower See *Centaurea cyanus*.

Cosmea See *Cosmos bipinnatus*.

Cotton Lavender See *Santolina*.

Cotton Thistle See *Onopordum acanthium*.

Creeping Fig See *Ficus pumila*.

Creeping Jenny See *Lysimachia nummularia*.

Crimson Glory Vine See *Vitis coignetiae*.

Crown of Thorns See *Euphorbia milii*.

Cupid's Dart See *Catananche caerulea*.

Curry Plant See *Helichrysum italicum*.

Cydonia See *Chaenomeles*.

Cypress See *Chamaecyparis*.

Daffodil See *Narcissus*.

Daisy Bush See *Olearia*.

Damson See *Prunus*, Damsons.

David's Harp See *Polygonatum* x *hybridum*.

Day Lily See *Hemerocallis*.

Devil's Ivy See *Epipremnum aureum*.

Dill See *Anethum graveolens*.

Dogwood See *Cornus sericea*.

Dove Tree See *Davidia involucrata*.

Drumstick Primula See *Primula denticulata*.

Dumb Cane See *Dieffenbachia*.

Dusty Miller See *Artemisia stelleriana*.

Dutch Lavender See *Lavandula vera*.

Dwarf Cornel See *Cornus canadensis*.

Dwarf Russian Almond See *Prunus tenella*.

Early Dutch Honeysuckle See *Lonicera periclymenum* 'Belgica'.

Edging Lobelia See *Lobelia erinus*.

Elder See *Sambucus*.

English Holly See *Ilex aquifolium*.

European Larch See *Larix decidua*.

European Wood Anemone See *Anemone nemorosa*.

Evening Primrose See *Oenothera trichocalyx*.

Everlasting Flower See *Xerochrysum bracteatum*.

Everlasting Sweet Pea See *Lathyrus latifolius*.

Fairy Primrose See *Primula malacoides*.

A–Z OF COMMON NAMES

Fairy Wallflower See *Erysimum alpinum*.

False Aralia See *Schefflera elegantissima*.

False Castor Oil Plant See *Fatsia japonica*.

Fennel See *Foeniculum vulgare*.

Feverfew See *Tanacetum parthenium*.

Fiddle-back Fig See *Ficus lyrata*.

Field Poppy See *Papaver rhoeas*.

Fir See *Picea*.

Firethorn See *Pyracantha*.

Flame Flower See *Tropaeolum speciosum*.

Flame Nettle See *Solenostemon scutellarioides*.

Flax See *Linum grandiflorum*.

Fleabane See *Erigeron speciosus*.

Florentine Iris See *Iris* 'Florentina'.

Florist's Anemone See *Anemone coronaria*.

Florist's Cineraria See *Pericallis* x *hybrida*.

Flowering Currant See *Ribes*.

Flowering Dogwood See *Cornus florida* and *Cornus kousa*.

Flowering Fern See *Osmunda regalis*.

Flowering Rush See *Butomus umbellatus*.

Flowering Tobacco Plant See *Nicotiana alata*.

Flower-of-an-hour See *Hibiscus trionum*.

Foam Flower See *Tiarella cordifolia*.

Foam of May See *Spiraea* 'Arguta'.

Forget-me-not See *Myosotis sylvatica*.

Foxglove See *Digitalis purpurea*.

Foxtail Lily See *Eremurus*.

Fremontia californica See *Fremontodendron californicum*.

French Hydrangea See *Hydrangea macrophylla*.

French Marigold See *Tagetes patula*.

French Tarragon See *Artemisia dracunculus* 'Sativa'.

Fuji Cherry See *Prunus incisa*.

Gage See *Prunus*, Gages.

Garden Flax See *Linum flavum*.

Garlic See *Allium sativum*.

Gayfeather See *Liatris*.

German Rampion See *Oenothera biennis*.

Ghost Tree See *Davidia involucrata*.

Giant Cowslip See *Primula florindae*.

Gladwyn See *Iris foetidissima*.

Globe Amaranth See *Gomphrena globosa*.

Globe Flower See *Trollius* x *cultorum*.

Glory of the Snow See *Chionodoxa*.

Gloxinia See *Sinningia speciosa*.

Goat-leaf Honeysuckle See *Lonicera caprifolium*.

Goat's Beard See *Aruncus diolcus*.

Gold Dust See *Aurinia saxatilis*.

Golden Bells See *Forsythia*.

Golden Chain Tree See *Laburnum*.

Golden Club See *Orontium aquaticum*.

Golden-leaved Hop See *Humulus lupulus* 'Aureus'

Golden Marguerite See *Anthemis punctata* subsp. *cupaniana*.

Golden Rain Tree See *Laburnum*.

Golden Rod See *Solidago* hybrids.

Gorse See *Ulex europaeus*.

Granny's Bonnet See *Aquilegia vulgaris*.

Grape Hyacinth See *Muscari armeniacum*.

Grape Ivy See *Cissus rhombifolia*.

Grape Vine See *Vitis vinifera*.

Greater Periwinkle See *Vinca major*.

Gromwell See *Lithodora diffusa*.

Gum Trees See *Eucalyptus*.

Hairy Canary Clover See *Lotus hirsutus*.

Handkerchief Tree See *Davidia involucrata*.

Hardy Fuchsia See *Fuchsia magellanica*.

Heath See *Erica*.

Heather See *Calluna vulgaris* and *Erica*.

Heliotrope See *Heliotropium arborescens*.

Hen-and-chicken Fern See *Asplenium bulbiferum*.

Hills of Snow See *Hydrangea arborescens*.

Himalayan Blue Poppy See *Meconopsis betonicifolia*.

Hollyhock See *Alcea rosea*.

Honesty See *Lunaria annua*.

Horseradish See *Armoracia rusticana*.

Hound's Tongue See *Cynoglossum amabile*.

Houseleek See *Sempervivum*.

Hyssop See *Hyssopus officinalis*.

Incense Cedar See *Calocedrus decurrens*.

Indian Bean Tree See *Catalpa bignonioides*.

Indian Pink See *Dianthus chinensis*.

Iron Cross Begonia See *Begonia masoniana*.

Ivy Tree See x *Fatshedera lizei*.

Japanese Anemone See *Anemone x hybrida*.

Japanese Cedar See *Cryptomeria japonica*.

Japanese Cherry See *Prunus*, Japanese Cherries.

Japanese Climbing Hydrangea See *Hydrangea anomala* subsp. *petiolaris*.

Japanese Crimson Glory Vine See *Vitis coignetiae*.

Japanese Honeysuckle See *Lonicera japonica*.

Japanese Primrose See *Primula japonica*.

Japanese Privet See *Ligustrum japonicum*.

Japanese Quince See *Chaenomeles*.

Japanese Spurge See *Pachysandra terminalis*.

Japanese Windflower See *Anemone x hybrida*.

Japanese Wisteria See *Wisteria floribunda*.

Japonica See *Chaenomeles*.

Jasmine Nightshade See *Solanum laxum*.

Jerusalem Cowslip See *Pulmonaria officinalis*.

Jerusalem Cross See *Lychnis chalcedonica*.

Jerusalem Sage See *Phlomis fruticosa*.

Jew's Mallow See *Kerria japonica*.

Joseph's Coat See *Amaranthus tricolor*.

Judas Tree See *Cercis siliquastrum*.

June Berry See *Amelanchier lamarckii*.

Kangaroo Vine See *Cissus antarctica*.

Katsura Tree See *Cercidiphyllum japonicum*.

Kingcup See *Caltha*.

Kingfisher Daisy See *Felicia bergeriana*.

Knotted Marjoram See *Origanum majorana*.

Lady's Eardrops See *Fuchsia*.

Lady's Mantle See *Alchemilla*.

Lamb's Ears See *Stachys byzantina*.

Lamb's Tongue See *Stachys byzantina*.

Large-flowered Mullein See *Verbascum densiflorum*.

Larkspur See *Consolida ajacis*.

Late Dutch Honeysuckle See *Lonicera periclymenum* 'Serotina'.

Lavender See *Lavandula angustifolia*.

Lenten Rose See *Helleborus orientalis*.

Lesser Periwinkle See *Vinca minor*.

Licorice Plant See *Helichrysum petiolare*.

Lily See *Lilium*.

Lily-of-the-Valley See *Convallaria majalis*.

Loosestrife See *Lysimachia*.

Lovage See *Levisticum officinale*.

Love-in-a-mist See *Nigella damascena*.

Love-lies-bleeding See *Amaranthus caudatus*.

Love Tree See *Cercis siliquastrum*.

Maidenhair Tree See *Ginkgo biloba*.

Maltese Cross See *Lychnis chalcedonica*.

M **P**

Maple See *Acer.*

Marsh Marigold See *Caltha.*

Marvel of Peru See *Mirabilis jalapa.*

Masterwort See *Astrantia.*

Matilija See *Romneya coulteri.*

Meadow Phlox See *Phlox maculata.*

Meadow Rue See *Thalictrum aquilegiifolium.*

Meadowsweet See *Filipendula purpurea.*

Mexican Aster See *Cosmos bipinnatus.*

Mexican Hat Plant See *Kalanchoe daigremontiana.*

Mexican Orange Blossom See *Choisya ternata.*

Mignonette See *Reseda odorata.*

Mile-a-minute-Vine See *Fallopia baldschuanica.*

Mint See *Mentha.*

Mistletoe Fig See *Ficus diversifolia.*

Mock Orange See *Philadelphus.*

Moneywort See *Lysimachia nummularia.*

Monkey Flower See *Mimulus.*

Monkey Puzzle See *Araucaria araucana.*

Monkshood See *Aconitum.*

Montbretia See *Crocosmia x crocosmiiflora.*

Moss Phlox See *Phlox subulata.*

Moss Pink See *Phlox subulata.*

Moth Mullein See *Verbascum blattaria.*

Mother Fern See *Asplenium bulbiferum.*

Mother-in-law's Tongue See *Sansevieria trifasciata.*

Mother of Thousands See *Saxifraga stolonifera.*

Mountain Dogwood See *Cornus nuttallii.*

Mountain Laurel See *Kalmia latifolia.*

Mount Wellington Peppermint See *Eucalyptus coccifera.*

Nasturtium See *Tropaeolum majus.*

Nectarine See *Prunus,* Nectarines.

Never Never Plant See *Ctenanthe oppenheimiana* 'Tricolor'

New Zealand Burr See *Acaena.*

New Zealand Flax See *Phormium tenax.*

New Zealand Hemp See *Phormium tenax.*

Night-scented Stock See *Matthiola bicornis.*

Norfolk Island Pine See *Araucaria heterophylla.*

Obedient Plant See *Physostegia virginiana.*

Old English Lavender See *Lavandula angustifolia.*

Oleaster See *Elaeagnus angustifolia.*

Opium Poppy See *Papaver somniferum.*

Orange-ball Tree See *Buddleja globosa.*

Oriental Bittersweet See *Celastrus orbiculatus.*

Oriental Poppy See *Papaver orientale.*

Ornamental Brambles See *Rubus.*

Ornamental Onions See *Allium.*

Orris Root See *Iris* 'Florentina'.

Oswego Tea See *Monarda didyma.*

Painted Nettle See *Solenostemon scutellarioides.*

Painted Tongue See *Salpiglossus sinuata.*

Pampas Grass See *Cortaderia selloana.*

Pansy See *Viola x wittrockiana.*

Parasol Plant See *Schefflera arboricola.*

Parsley See *Petroselinum crispum.*

Pasque Flower See *Pulsatilla vulgaris.*

Passion Flower See *Passiflora.*

Peach See *Prunus,* Peaches.

Pearl Everlasting See *Anaphalis.*

Perennial Flax See *Linum perenne.*

Perennial Phlox See *Phlox paniculata.*

Persian Candytuft See *Aethionema.*

Peruvian Lily See *Alstroemeria.*

Pheasant's Eye See *Adonis aestivalis*.

Pick-a-back-Plant See *Tolmiea menziesii*.

Pickerel Plant See *Pontederia cordata*.

Pincushion Plant See *Cotula barbata*.

Pine See *Pinus*.

Pink Jasmine See *Jasminum polyanthum*.

Pink Sandwort See *Arenaria purpurascens*.

Plantain Lily See *Hosta*.

Plum See *Prunus*, Plums.

Plume Poppy See *Macleaya*.

Poached Egg Plant See *Limnanthes douglasii*.

Poet's Jessamine See *Jasminum officinale*.

Poinsettia See *Euphorbia pulcherrima*.

Poker Plant See *Kniphofia*.

Polyanthus See *Primula* Pruhonicensis Hybrids.

Poor Man's Orchid See *Schizanthus pinnatus*.

Portugal Laurel See *Prunus lusitanica*.

Pot Marigold See *Calendula officinalis*.

Pouch Flower See *Calceolaria* × *herbeohybrida* and *Calceolaria integrifolia*.

Primrose See *Primula vulgaris*.

Primrose Jasmine See *Jasminum mesnyi*.

Prince of Wales Feather See *Celosia argentea* var. *plumosa*.

Prince's Feather See *Amaranthus hypochondriacus*.

Purple Cockle See *Agrostemma githago* 'Milas'.

Purple Cone Flower See *Echinacea purpurea*.

Purple Flag Iris See *Iris germanica*.

Purple Loosestrife See *Lythrum salicaria*.

Purple Mullein See *Verbascum phoeniceum*.

Quamash See *Camassia quamash*.

Queen Anne's Lace See *Trachelium caeruleum*.

Rat's-tail Cactus See *Aporocactus flagelliformis*.

Red-barked Dogwood See *Cornus alba*.

Rex Begonia See *Begonia rex*.

Rock Cress See *Arabis alpina* subsp. *caucasica*.

Rock Rose See *Cistus* and *Helianthemum*.

Rose See *Rosa*.

Rose of Sharon See *Hypericum* 'Hidcote'.

Rosemary See *Rosmarinus officinalis*.

Royal Fern See *Osmunda regalis*.

Rubber Plant See *Ficus elastica*.

Rue See *Ruta graveolens*.

Russian Sage See *Perovskia atriplicifolia*.

Russian Vine See *Fallopia baldschuanica*.

Sage See *Salvia officinalis*.

Sandwort See *Arenaria purpurescens*.

Scarlet Flax See *Linum grandiflorum* 'Rubrum'.

Scarlet Pimpernel See *Anagallis arvensis*.

Scarlet Sage See *Salvia splendens*.

Scotch Thistle See *Onopordum acanthium*.

Sea Lavender See *Limonium latifolium* and *Limonium sinuatum*.

Sedge See *Carex*.

Self-heal See *Prunella*.

Shasta Daisy See *Leucanthemum maximum*.

Sheep Laurel See *Kalmia angustifolia*.

Shoo Fly Plant See *Nicandra physalodes*.

Shrimp Plant See *Justicia brandegeeana*.

Shrubby Cinquefoil See *Potentilla fruticosa*.

Shrubby Mallow See *Hibiscus syriacus*.

Shrubby Veronica See *Hebe*.

Siberian Iris See *Iris sibirica*.

Siberian Wallflower See *Erysimum* × *allionii*.

Signet Marigold See *Tagetes tenuifolia*.

Silver Berry See *Elaeagnus commutata*.

A–Z OF COMMON NAMES

S | **T**

Silver Fir See *Abies*.

Silver Lace See *Tanacetum ptarmiciflorum*.

Skunk Cabbage See *Lysichiton*.

Slipper Flower See *Calceolaria x herbeohybrida* and *Calceolaria integrifolia*.

Sloe See *Prunus spinosa*.

Snakeweed See *Persicaria bistorta* 'Superba'.

Snapdragon See *Antirrhinum majus*.

Sneezewort See *Helenium autumnale*.

Snowberry See *Symphoricarpos*.

Snowflake See *Leucojum*.

Snow-in-summer See *Cerastium tomentosum*.

Snow on the Mountain See *Euphorbia marginata*.

Snowy Mespilus See *Amelanchier lamarckii*.

Solomon's Seal See *Polygonatum x hybridum*.

Southernwood See *Artemisia abrotanum*.

Spanish Bluebell See *Hyacinthoides hispanica*.

Spanish Broom See *Spartium junceum*.

Speedwell See *Veronica*.

Spider Flower See *Cleome spinosa*.

Spider Plant See *Chlorophytum comosum*.

Spiderwort See *Tradescantia x andersoniana*.

Spotted Laurel See *Aucuba japonica*.

Spring Starflower See *Ipheion uniflorum*.

Spruce See *Picea*.

Squill See *Scilla*.

Staff Vine See *Celastrus orbiculatus*.

Stag's Horn Sumach See *Rhus typhina*.

St Bernard's Lily See *Anthericum liliago*.

Stinking Iris See *Iris foetidissima*.

St John's Wort See *Hypericum* 'Hidcote'.

Stock See *Matthiola incana*.

Strawberry Geranium See *Saxifraga stolonifera*.

Summer Cypress See *Bassia scoparia* f. *trichophylla*.

Summer Lilac See *Buddleja davidii*.

Summer Phlox See *Phlox paniculata*.

Summer Savory See *Satureja hortensis*.

Sunflower See *Helianthus annuus*.

Sun Plant See *Portulaca grandiflora*.

Sun Rose See *Cistus* and *Helianthemum*.

Swamp Cypress See *Taxodium distichum*.

Swan River Daisy See *Brachyscome iberidifolia*.

Swedish Ivy See *Plectranthus coleoides* 'Marginatus'.

Sweet Alyssum See *Lobularia maritima*.

Sweet Bay See *Laurus nobilis*.

Sweet Bergamot See *Monarda didyma*.

Sweet Cicely See *Myrrhis odorata*.

Sweet Gum See *Liquidambar styraciflua*.

Sweetheart Plant See *Philodendron scandens*.

Sweet Marjoram See *Origanum majorana*.

Sweet Pea See *Lathyrus odoratus*.

Sweet Rocket See *Hesperis matronalis*.

Sweet Scabious See *Scabiosa atropurpurea*.

Sweet Sultan See *Centaurea moschata*.

Sweet William See *Dianthus barbatus*.

Swiss Cheese Plant See *Monstera deliciosa*.

Tamarisk See *Tamarix*.

Tansy See *Tanacetum vulgare*.

Tarragon See *Artemisia dracunculus*.

Tassel Flower See *Emilia coccinea*.

Thrift See *Armeria*.

Thyme See *Thymus*.

Tickseed See *Coreopsis tinctoria*.

Ti-palm See *Cordyline fruticosa*.

Toadflax See *Linaria maroccana*.

Touch-me-not See *Impatiens balsamina*.

Trailing Fig See *Ficus radicans*.

Trailing Lobelia See *Lobelia erinus*.

Transvaal Daisy See *Gerbera jamesonii*.

Tree Lavatera See *Lavatera x clementii* 'Rosea'.

Tree Lupin See *Lupinus arboreus*.

Tree Poppy See *Romneya coulteri*.

Tricoloured Chrysanthemum See *Chrysanthemum carinatum*.

Trinity Flower See *Tradescantia x andersoniana*.

Tulip See *Tulipa*.

Tulip Tree See *Liriodendron tulipifera*.

Turtle Head See *Chelone*.

Umbrella Tree See *Schefflera actinophylla*.

Urn Plant See *Aechmea*.

Valerian See *Centranthus ruber*.

Variegated Buffalo Grass See *Stenotaphrum secundatum* 'Variegatum'.

Variegated Canary Island Ivy See *Hedera canariensis* 'Gloire de Marengo'.

Variegated Gout Weed See *Aegopodium podagraria* 'Variegatum'.

Variegated Ground Elder See *Aegopodium podagraria* 'Variegatum'.

Variegated Ground Ivy See *Glechoma hederacea* 'Variegata'.

Variegated Persian Ivy See *Hedera colchica* 'Dentata Variegata'.

Variegated Reed Sweetgrass See *Glyceria maxima* var. *variegata*.

Variegated Sweet Flag See *Acorus calamus* 'Argenteostriatus'.

Verbena See *Verbena x hybrida*.

Violet Cress See *Ionopsidium acaule*.

Viper's Bugloss See *Echium plantagineum*.

Virginia Stock See *Malcolmia maritima*.

Wallflower See *Erysimum cheiri*.

Wall Rock Cress See *Arabis alpina* subsp. *caucasica*.

Wandering Jew See *Tradescantia fluminensis*.

Water Gladiolus See *Butomus umbellatus*.

Water Hawthorn See *Aponogeton distachyos*.

Waterlily See *Nymphaea*.

Wattle See *Acacia*.

Wax Begonia See *Begonia semperflorens*.

Wax Ivy See *Senecio macroglossus*.

Weeping Fig See *Ficus benjamina*.

Welsh Poppy See *Meconopsis cambrica*.

Western Red Cedar See *Thuja plicata*.

White-leaf Everlasting See *Helichrysum italicum*.

White Mugwort See *Artemisia lactiflora*.

White Sage See *Artemisia ludoviciana*.

Wild Sweet William See *Phlox maculata*.

Winter Aconite See *Eranthis hyemalis*.

Winter-flowering Jasmine See *Jasminum nudiflorum*.

Winter Savory See *Satureja montana*.

Witch Hazel See *Hamamelis*.

Wood Anemone See *Anemone nemorosa*.

Woodruff See *Asperula odorata*.

Woolly Mullein See *Verbascum phlomoides*.

Yarrow See *Achillea*.

Yellow European Hop See *Humulus lupulus* 'Aureus'.

Yellow Flag Iris See *Iris pseudacorus*.

Yellow-leaved Chinese Honeysuckle See *Lonicera nitida* 'Baggeson's Gold'.

Yellow Water Lily See *Nuphar lutea*.

Yew See *Taxus baccata*.

Youth-on-age See *Tolmiea menziesii*.

Zebra Plant See *Aphelandra squarrosa*.

How to propagate plants

Plants are mainly arranged by their botanical names (see pages 42–50 for an index of common names). Some entries, however, encompass a group of botanically related plants – for example, bamboos. After each name, there is a short description of the type of plant and its growth habit. By necessity, this list is not comprehensive, but all the most commonly grown house and garden plants are included. Where details such as the best time to sow seeds or layer a plant are not specified in an entry, you should follow the general advice given in the relevant method section (see pages 8–41).

A   A–Z OF PROPAGATING PLANTS   A

Abelia Hardy semi-evergreen or deciduous shrubs – in mid-summer take 7.5 cm (3 in) long half-ripe cuttings and insert in pots placed in gentle warmth, or in a cold frame.

Abies (Silver Fir) Hardy evergreen conifers – during late winter sow seeds in pots and place in a cold frame.

Abutilon Wide range of perennials, shrubs and small trees – most species can be raised from 7.5 cm (3 in) long half-ripe cuttings taken from lateral shoots in summer and placed in gentle warmth.

Abutilon vitifolium is best raised from seeds sown in warmth in mid- and late spring and placed in a warm greenhouse; other abutilons (except variegated and named forms) can also be raised from seeds.

Acacia (Wattle) Tender deciduous and evergreen trees and shrubs – during mid-summer take 5–10 cm (2–4 in) long half-ripe cuttings, preferably with a heel, of *A. paradoxa* (syn. *A. armata*) and *A. longifolia*. Place them in gentle warmth. For other species, sow seeds in mid-spring and place in gentle warmth in a greenhouse.

Acaena (New Zealand Burr) Hardy herbaceous perennials – during autumn or spring lift and divide congested plants. Alternatively, in late winter sow seeds in pots placed in a cold frame.

Acanthus mollis (Bear's Breeches) Hardy herbaceous perennial – lift and divide congested plants in autumn or spring. Alternatively, sow seeds in spring in pots and place in a cold frame.

Acanthus spinosus (Bear's Breeches) Hardy herbaceous perennial – lift and divide congested plants in autumn or spring. Alternatively, sow seeds in spring in pots and place in a cold frame.

Acer

Acer (Maple) Hardy deciduous trees and shrubs – sow seeds in early or mid-autumn in seed-trays (flats) and place in a cold frame. Named forms must be grafted or budded in mid-spring.

Achillea (Yarrow) Herbaceous perennial – lift and divide congested plants in autumn or spring. Alternatively, in spring sow seeds in seed-trays (flats) and place in a cold frame.

Achimenes Deciduous greenhouse perennials – in early spring separate and replant young tubers from dried-off plants.

Acidanthera bicolor See *Gladiolus*.

Aconitum (Monkshood) Hardy herbaceous perennials – lift and divide congested plants in autumn or spring. Alternatively, in spring sow seeds in seed-trays (flats) and place in a cold frame.

Acorus calamus 'Argenteostriatus' (Variegated Sweet Flag) Hardy evergreen perennial – in spring lift and divide congested clumps.

Actinidia Hardy deciduous climbing shrub with a twining habit – during mid- and late summer take 7.5–10 cm (3–4 in) long half-ripe cuttings and place in gentle warmth. Alternatively, sow seeds in mid-autumn in seed-trays (flats) and place them in a cold frame.

Adiantum Hardy and tender ferns – in spring lift and divide congested plants. Alternatively, in early spring sow spores (see Glossary).

Adonis aestivalis (Pheasant's Eye) Hardy annual – sow 6 mm (¼ in) deep.

Aechmea (Urn Plant) Evergreen terrestrial or epiphytic greenhouse or house plants – use a sharp knife to cut 10–13 cm (4–5 in) long sideshoots close to the plant's base. Allow the cut surfaces to dry for a day, then insert in equal parts moist peat and sharp sand and place in gentle warmth. Sometimes, it is necessary to support plants with thin stakes.

Aegopodium podagraria 'Variegatum' (Variegated Gout Weed, Variegated Ground Elder) Rhizomatous-rooted perennial – during spring lift and divide congested plants.

Aethionema (Persian Candytuft) Hardy evergreen perennials – during mid-spring sow seeds in pots and place in a cold frame.

Aethionema 'Warley Rose'
Hardy evergreen perennial – in early or mid-summer take 5 cm (2 in) long softwood cuttings from non-flowering shoots. Insert them in pots and place in gentle warmth.

Agapanthus (African Lily)
Half-hardy and hardy evergreen perennials with fleshy roots – in spring divide congested plants, just as growth begins. It can also be increased from seeds sown in spring in gentle warmth, but it takes up to three years for plants to flower.

Agave
Tender, succulent, rosette-forming perennials – during early summer remove offsets from around rosettes, pot up and place in gentle warmth. Alternatively, during spring sow seeds in pots and place in gentle warmth.

Agave victoriae-reginae
Succulent rosette-forming greenhouse and house plant – during spring sow seeds in pots and place in gentle warmth.

Ageratum
Half-hardy annual – sow 3 mm (⅛ in) deep.

Aglaonema
Evergreen perennial greenhouse and house plant – in spring divide congested plants. Alternatively, in spring sow seeds in gentle warmth. Also, remove basal sucker-like shoots – pot up and place in gentle warmth.

Agrostemma githago 'Milas'
(Corn Cockle, Purple Cockle) Hardy annual – sow 6 mm (¼ in) deep.

Ajuga (Bugle)
Hardy herbaceous perennial – lift and divide congested plants in autumn or early spring. Replant the young pieces.

Alcea rosea (Hollyhock)
Hardy perennial usually grown as a biennial – sow 12 mm (½ in) deep.

Alchemilla
(Lady's Mantle) Hardy herbaceous perennials – lift and divide congested plants in autumn or early spring. Replant young pieces from around the outside of the clump. It produces self-sown seedlings, which can be lifted and transplanted in late summer.

Allium
(Ornamental Onions) Hardy bulbs – in autumn or spring lift and divide congested clumps. Many species can be raised from seeds – between autumn and spring sow thinly in pots placed in a cold frame.

Allium sativum (Garlic)
Hardy bulbous perennial – during late summer lift and divide existing bulbs; use most for culinary purposes, but retain some for replanting during the following late winter.

Allium schoenoprasum (Chives)
Hardy bulbous perennial – in autumn or spring lift and divide congested plants.

Aloe
Succulent greenhouse perennials or house plants – during summer remove offsets (allow to dry for a couple of days) and pot up.

Alstroemeria
(Peruvian Lily) Hardy or slightly tender fleshy-rooted herbaceous perennials – lift and divide congested plants in autumn or spring. Try to form clusters about 10 cm (4 in) wide, without disturbing too much soil.

Althaea rosea
See *Alcea rosea*.

Alyssum maritimum
See *Lobularia maritima*.

Alyssum saxatile
See *Aurinia saxatilis*.

Amaranthus caudatus
(Love-lies-bleeding) Hardy annual – sow 3 mm (⅛ in) deep. Alternatively, raise as a half-hardy annual – sow 3 mm (⅛ in) deep.

Amaranthus hypochondriacus
(Prince's Feather) Half-hardy annual – sow 3 mm (⅛ in) deep.

Amaranthus tricolor
(Joseph's Coat) Half-hardy annual – sow 3 mm (⅛ in) deep.

Amaryllis belladonna
(Belladonna Lily) Slightly tender bulbous plant – during summer (when the leaves turn yellow) lift, divide and replant.

Amelanchier lamarckii

Amelanchier lamarckii
(June Berry, Snowy Mespilus) Hardy deciduous large shrub or small tree – during late summer layer low-growing stems. Alternatively, in spring or autumn detach rooted suckers and plant them in a nursery bed until large enough to be planted in a border.

Anagallis arvensis
(Scarlet Pimpernel) Hardy annual – sow 6 mm (¼ in) deep.

Anaphalis
(Pearl Everlasting) Hardy herbaceous perennials – lift and divide congested plants in early autumn or spring.

Anchusa azurea
Herbaceous perennial – lift and divide congested plants in autumn or spring. Alternatively, take root cuttings.

Anchusa italica
See *Anchusa azurea*.

A–Z OF PROPAGATING PLANTS

Anemone blanda Slightly tender tuber – lift and carefully divide congested plants after the leaves die down.

Anemone coronaria (Florist's Anemone) Slightly tender tuber – lift and carefully divide congested plants after the leaves have died down.

Anemone x hybrida (Japanese Anemone, Japanese Windflower) Hardy herbaceous perennial – lift and divide congested plants in autumn or spring. Alternatively, take root cuttings in winter.

Anemone nemorosa (European Wood Anemone, Wood Anemone) Hardy tuberous-rooted plant – when the flowers fade, lift and carefully divide congested plants, setting the tubers about 3.5 cm (1½ in) deep.

Anethum graveolens (Dill) Hardy annual – sow 12 mm (½ in) deep.

Angelica archangelica (Angelica) Hardy biennial – sow 12 mm (½ in) deep.

Anthemis cupaniana See Anthemis punctata subsp. cupaniana.

Anthemis punctata subsp. **cupaniana** (Golden Marguerite) Short-lived herbaceous perennial – during spring lift and divide congested plants. Alternatively, in early summer take 5–7.5 cm (2–3 in) long cuttings and insert in pots placed in a cold frame.

Anthericum liliago (St Bernard's Lily) Hardy herbaceous perennial – in autumn or spring lift and divide congested plants. Alternatively, in early spring sow seeds in pots placed in a cold frame.

Anthriscus cerefolium (Chervil) Hardy biennial – sow 12 mm (½ in) deep.

Anthurium – Evergreen greenhouse and house plants – during spring divide and repot congested plants.

Antirrhinum majus (Snapdragon) Hardy perennial, hardy annual (sow 6 mm (¼ in) deep) or half-hardy annual (sow 3 mm (⅛ in) deep).

Aphelandra squarrosa (Zebra Plant) Tender evergreen greenhouse or house plant – after the flowers fade, cut the main stem to just above a pair of healthy leaves to encourage the development of shoots that later can be used as cuttings. Cut them off when 10 cm (4 in) long and insert in pots placed in gentle warmth.

Aponogeton distachyos

Aponogeton distachyos (Cape Asparagus, Cape Pondweed, Water Hawthorn) Hardy aquatic – during spring lift and divide congested plants.

Aporocactus flagelliformis (Rat's-tail Cactus) Tender cactus for greenhouse and house display – during spring sow seeds in pots and place in gentle warmth. Alternatively, in late spring and early summer take cuttings (allow to dry for a couple of days) and insert in pots placed in gentle warmth.

Aquilegia vulgaris (Columbine, Granny's Bonnet) Hardy herbaceous perennial – lift and divide congested plants in autumn or spring. Alternatively, raise it as a half-hardy annual – sow 3 mm (⅛ in) deep – or hardy biennial – sow 6 mm (¼ in) deep.

Arabis alpina subsp. **caucasica** (Rock Cress, Wall Rock Cress) Hardy evergreen perennial – during early autumn lift and divide congested plants. Alternatively, during early and mid-summer take 5 cm (2 in) long cuttings from non-flowering shoots and insert in sandy compost in pots placed in a cold frame.

Arabis blepharophylla Slightly tender evergreen perennial often grown in an alpine house in cold areas – during early and mid-summer take 5 cm (2 in) long cuttings from non-flowering shoots and insert in sandy compost in pots placed in a cold frame. Alternatively, during mid-summer sow seeds in pots placed in a cold frame.

Arabis caucasica See Arabis alpina subsp. caucasica.

Arabis ferdinandi-coburgi Hardy evergreen perennial – during early and mid-summer take cuttings from non-flowering shoots and insert in sandy compost in pots placed in a cold frame.

Araucaria araucana

Araucaria araucana (Chile Pine, Monkey Puzzle) Evergreen conifer – in spring sow seeds singly in pots and place in a cold frame. Alternatively, in mid-summer take 10 cm (4 in) long cuttings from vertical shoots and insert in pots placed in a cold frame.

Araucaria excelsa See Araucaria heterophylla.

Araucaria heterophylla (Norfolk Island Pine) Evergreen conifer, grown in temperate climates in its juvenile form as a house plant or in a greenhouse – in early and mid-spring sow seeds singly in pots and place in gentle warmth. Alternatively, in late winter cut back leggy plants to create cuttings; when large enough, take 7.5 cm (3 in) long shoots and insert in pots in gentle warmth.

Araucaria imbricata See *Araucaria araucana*.

Arbutus Hardy and half-hardy evergreen trees and shrubs – during mid-summer take 7.5–10 cm (3–4 in) long half-ripe cuttings and insert in pots placed in a cold frame. Alternatively, many species can be raised by sowing seeds in early autumn and placed in a cold frame.

Arctostaphylos Hardy evergreen shrubs – during spring layer low-growing branches. Alternatively, during mid- and late summer take 5–7.5 cm (2–3 in) long heel cuttings from lateral shoots and insert in pots placed in a cold frame.

Arctotis x hybrida (African Daisy) Half-hardy annual – sow 6 mm (¼ in) deep.

Arenaria balearica Sub-shrubby evergreen – during spring lift and divide congested clumps.

Arenaria montana Sub-shrubby evergreen – during early and mid-summer take 2.5–5 cm (1–2 in) long cuttings from non-flowering basal shoots and insert in pots placed in a cold frame.

Arenaria purpurascens (Pink Sandwort, Sandwort) Hardy rock-garden perennial – during spring lift and divide congested plants.

Armeria (Thrift) Hardy evergreen perennial – during spring lift and divide congested plants.

Armoracia rusticana (Horseradish) Hardy herbaceous perennial – during early winter lift and store the remaining roots in boxes of sand ready for replanting in late winter.

Artemisia abrotanum (Southernwood) Hardy deciduous or semi-evergreen shrub – during late summer take 7.5–10 cm (3–4 in) long half-ripe heel cuttings and insert in pots placed in a cold frame.

Artemisia absinthium (Common Wormwood) Hardy sub-shrubby and deciduous – during late summer take 7.5–10 cm (3–4 in) long half-ripe heel cuttings and insert in pots placed in a cold frame.

Artemisia arborescens Slightly tender deciduous or semi-evergreen shrub – during late summer take 7.5–10 cm (3–4 in) long half-ripe heel cuttings and insert in pots placed in a cold frame.

Artemisia dracunculus (Tarragon) Hardy perennial – during early and mid-spring lift and divide congested plants.

***Artemisia dracunculus* 'Sativa'** (French Tarragon) Moderately hardy perennial – during early and mid-spring lift and divide congested plants.

Artemisia lactiflora (White Mugwort) Hardy herbaceous perennial – during autumn or spring lift and divide congested plants.

Artemisia ludoviciana (White Sage) Hardy herbaceous perennial – during autumn or spring lift and divide congested plants.

Artemisia stelleriana (Dusty Miller) Hardy herbaceous perennial – during autumn or spring lift and divide congested plants. Alternatively, during mid- and late summer take 7.5 cm (3 in) long half-ripe heel cuttings and insert in pots placed in a cold frame.

Aruncus dioicus (Goat's Beard) Hardy herbaceous perennial – lift and divide congested plants in autumn.

Asperula odorata (Woodruff) Hardy herbaceous perennial – lift and divide congested plants during autumn or spring.

Asperula orientalis (Annual Woodruff) Hardy annual – sow 6 mm (¼ in) deep.

Aspidistra elatior (Cast Iron Plant) Evergreen greenhouse or house plant – during spring divide congested plants.

Asplenium (Spleenwort) Hardy and tender evergreen ferns – raise new plants from spores (see Glossary).

Asplenium bulbiferum (Hen-and-chicken Fern, Mother Fern) Tender evergreen fern – detach young bulbils from the fronds and press into compost in pots placed in gentle warmth.

Aster Hardy herbaceous perennials – lift and divide congested plants in autumn or spring. Lift and divide late autumn-flowering types, such as the Michaelmas Daisy, in early spring.

Astilbe x arendsii Hardy herbaceous perennial – lift and divide congested plants in spring.

Astrantia (Masterwort) Hardy herbaceous perennials – lift and divide congested plants in autumn or spring.

Astrophytum Tender cacti – in spring sow seeds in pots placed in gentle warmth.

Athyrium Hardy and tender ferns – in spring lift and divide congested plants, or raise from spores (see Glossary).

Aubrieta deltoidea Low-growing evergreen perennial – in late summer or early autumn lift and divide congested plants. Alternatively, sow seeds 6 mm (¼ in) deep in seed drills in a nursery bed from mid-spring to early autumn.

Aucuba japonica

Aucuba japonica (Spotted Laurel) Hardy evergreen shrub – during late summer and early autumn take 10–13 cm (4–5 in) long heel cuttings from lateral shoots and insert in pots placed in a cold frame.

A–Z OF PROPAGATING PLANTS

A   **B**

Aurinia saxatilis (Gold Dust) Shrubby evergreen perennial – during summer take 5–7.5 cm (2–3 in) long cuttings and insert in pots placed in a cold frame.

Ballota pseudodictamnus Hardy deciduous sub-shrub – in late summer and early autumn take 7.5–10 cm (3–4 in) long cuttings from non-flowering lateral shoots and insert in pots placed in a cold frame.

Bamboos Hardy evergreen cane-like plants – there are several vegetative ways to increase them:

• **Division of clumps** – in late spring dig up clumps without causing excessive damage to the roots and carefully divide them. Large parts can be replanted directly in a border, and small ones in a nursery bed. Do not allow the roots to become dry.

• **Rhizome cuttings** – in mid-spring dig up the roots of species with 'running' roots. Cut the rhizomes into pieces about 15 cm (6 in) long and insert them vertically into a narrow trench in a nursery bed. The tip should be positioned just above the soil's surface. A year or so later, move the rooted rhizomes to their permanent positions. Incidentally, this method of increasing bamboos is less strenuous than digging up and dividing the entire clump.

• **Basal cane cuttings** – this is ideal for bamboos that do not have long 'running' roots and instead form clumps. In mid- to late spring pull soil away from the side of a clump and expose rhizomes at the base of a two-year-old cane. Cut down the cane to 30 cm (1 ft) of its base and lift the roots with as much soil as possible attached to them. Plant the roots and base of the cane in a deep pot or box and place in gentle warmth. Keep the compost moist. Again, this is simpler and easier than digging up entire clumps.

Bassia scoparia f. trichophylla (Burning Bush, Summer Cypress) Hardy annual – sow 6 mm (¼ in) deep. Can also be raised as a half-hardy annual – sow 3 mm (⅛ in) deep.

Begonia masoniana (Iron Cross Begonia) Tender rhizomatous begonia – during spring and early summer divide congested plants. Alternatively, during late spring and early summer take leaf cuttings.

Begonia rex (Rex Begonia) Tender rhizomatous begonia – during late spring and early summer divide congested plants. Alternatively, during spring and early summer take leaf cuttings.

Begonia semperflorens (Wax Begonia) Greenhouse perennial invariably grown as a half-hardy annual – sow the small seeds on the surface of compost.

Begonia x tuberhybrida Tender tuberous-rooted plants – during early and mid spring put healthy tubers into boxes of moist peat. As soon as they develop shoots cut up the tubers into several pieces – each must have at least one healthy shoot. Alternatively, use 7.5 cm (3 in) long shoots as cuttings and insert in pots placed in gentle warmth.

Bellis perennis (Common Daisy) Hardy perennial usually grown as a biennial – sow 6 mm (¼ in) deep.

Beloperone guttata See *Justicia brandegeeana*.

Berberis

Berberis (Barberry) Hardy evergreen and deciduous shrubs – from autumn to spring divide suckering species. Alternatively, in late summer or early autumn take 7.5–10 cm (3–4 in) long heel cuttings and insert in pots placed in a cold frame.

Bergenia Hardy herbaceous perennials – lift and divide congested plants in autumn or spring.

Betula (Birch) Hardy deciduous trees and shrubs – during early and mid-spring sow seeds in pots and place in a cold frame. Forms of *Betula pendula* are grafted in spring.

Billbergia Tender evergreen greenhouse and house plants – when half the size of a full-grown plant, remove sucker-like sideshoots (allow the cut ends to dry for a few days) and insert in pots placed in gentle warmth.

Blackberry Deciduous shrub with long, spine-clad stems – tip-layer long stems in late summer or early autumn.

Borago officinalis (Borage) Hardy annual – sow 3–6 mm (⅛–¼ in) deep.

Bougainvillea Tender deciduous greenhouse plant – during summer take 7.5 cm (3 in) long half-ripe cuttings and insert in pots placed in gentle warmth.

Brachyglottis 'Sunshine' Evergreen shrub – during late summer layer low-growing stems. Alternatively, in late summer take 7.5 cm (3 in) long cuttings from the current season's growth and insert in pots placed in a cold frame.

Brachyscome iberidifolia (Swan River Daisy) Half-hardy annual – sow 3 mm (⅛ in) deep.

Brassaia actinophylla See *Schefflera actinophylla*.

Brunnera macrophylla Hardy herbaceous perennial – during autumn or spring lift and divide congested plants.

Buddleja alternifolia Hardy deciduous shrub – in mid-summer take 10–13 cm (4–5 in) long half-ripe heel cuttings and insert in pots placed in a cold frame.

Buddleja crispa Half-hardy deciduous shrub – in mid-summer take 10–13 cm (4–5 in) long half-ripe heel cuttings and insert in pots placed in a cold frame.

Buddleja davidii

Buddleja davidii (Butterfly Bush, Summer Lilac) Hardy deciduous shrub – in mid-summer take 10–13 cm (4–5 in) long half-ripe heel cuttings and insert in pots placed in a cold frame. Alternatively, in autumn take 25–30 cm (10–12 in) long hardwood cuttings and insert vertically 20 cm (8 in) deep in a nursery bed.

Buddleja fallowiana Half-hardy deciduous shrub – in mid-summer take 10–13 cm (4–5 in) long half-ripe heel cuttings and insert in pots placed in a cold frame.

Buddleja globosa (Orange-ball Tree) Slightly tender evergreen or semi-evergreen shrub – in mid-summer take 10–13 cm (4–5 in) long half-ripe heel cuttings and insert in pots placed in a cold frame.

Bupleurum fruticosa Evergreen or semi-evergreen shrub – take half-ripe cuttings, with heels.

Butomus umbellatus (Flowering Rush, Water Gladiolus) Hardy semi-aquatic – during spring lift and divide congested plants.

Buxus sempervirens (Common Box) Hardy evergreen shrub – during late summer and early autumn take 7.5–10 cm (3–4 in) long cuttings and insert in pots in a cold frame.

Caladium Tender, tuberous-rooted greenhouse perennials – during spring, when being repotted, detach and repot young tubers.

Calathea Tender greenhouse perennials – during early summer divide congested plants, repot and place in gentle warmth.

Calceolaria x herbeohybrida (Pouch Flower, Slipper Flower) Greenhouse biennial usually grown as a half-hardy annual – just press the seeds into the compost's surface.

Calceolaria integrifolia (Pouch Flower, Slipper Flower) Half-hardy perennial usually grown as a half-hardy annual – just press the seeds into the compost's surface.

Calendula officinalis (Pot Marigold) Hardy annual – sow 12 mm (½ in) deep.

Callicarpa Hardy deciduous shrubs and small trees – during mid- and late summer take 7.5–10 cm (3–4 in) long heel cuttings and insert in pots placed in gentle warmth.

Callistemon (Bottle Brush) Hardy and half-hardy evergreen trees and shrubs – in mid- and late summer take 7.5–10 cm (3–4 in) long half-ripe heel cuttings and insert in pots placed in gentle warmth.

Callistephus chinensis (China Aster) Half-hardy annual – sow 6 mm (¼ in) deep.

Calluna vulgaris (Heather) Low-growing evergreen shrub – during mid- and late summer take 2.5–5 cm (1–2 in) long cuttings from sideshoots. Remove lower leaves and insert about 18 mm (¾ in) deep in pots. Place in gentle warmth.

Calocedrus decurrens (Incense Cedar) Hardy evergreen conifer – in late autumn sow seeds in pots and place in a cold frame or cool greenhouse. Alternatively, from mid-summer to early autumn take 7.5 cm (3 in) long cuttings and insert in pots in a cold frame. The variegated form, *C. decurrens* 'Aureo-variegata', must be increased from cuttings.

Caltha (Kingcup, Marsh Marigold) Hardy herbaceous perennials – during late spring or early summer lift and divide congested plants.

Camassia quamash (Camass, Quamash) Bulbous herbaceous perennial – lift and divide congested clumps in autumn. Replant large bulbs but place small ones in a nursery bed for 2–3 years.

Camellia Hardy evergreen shrub – in mid- and late summer take 7.5–10 cm (3–4 in) long cuttings and insert in pots placed in gentle warmth. Alternatively, in autumn layer long shoots. Leaf-bud cuttings can be taken from early to late summer.

Campanula (Bellflowers) Herbaceous forms with clustered stems can be lifted and divided in autumn or spring. Alternatively, in spring take 3.5–5 cm (1½–2 in) long cuttings from non-flowering basal shoots. Several forms can be raised from seeds sown during spring or early summer and placed in gentle warmth or a cold frame.

Campanula medium (Canterbury Bell) Hardy biennial – sow 6 mm (¼ in) deep.

Carex (Sedge) Grass-like, rhizomatous-rooted perennials – during spring lift and divide congested plants.

A–Z OF PROPAGATING PLANTS

C   **C**

Carpenteria californica

Carpenteria californica Hardy evergreen shrub – during spring sow seeds in pots and place in gentle warmth.

Carum carvi (Caraway) Hardy biennial – sow 6 mm (¼ in) deep.

Caryopteris x clandonensis (Bluebeard) Hardy deciduous shrub – during late summer or early autumn take 7.5–10 cm (3–4 in) long half-ripe cuttings and insert in pots placed in a cold frame.

Catalpa bignonioides (Indian Bean Tree) Hardy deciduous tree – during mid- and late summer take 7.5–10 cm (3–4 in) long half-ripe heel cuttings and insert in pots placed in gentle warmth.

Catananche caerulea (Cupid's Dart) Short-lived herbaceous perennial – in spring take root cuttings. Alternatively, sow seeds 6 mm (¼ in) deep in spring in pots and place in a cold frame.

Ceanothus 'Burkwoodii' (Californian Lilac) Hardy evergreen shrub – in mid-summer take 7.5 cm (3 in) long semi-ripe cuttings and insert in pots placed in gentle warmth.

Ceanothus 'Cascade' (Californian Lilac) Half-hardy evergreen shrub – in mid-summer take 7.5 cm (3 in) long semi-ripe cuttings and insert in pots placed in gentle warmth.

Ceanothus 'Delight' (Californian Lilac) Hardy evergreen shrub – in mid-summer take 7.5 cm (3 in) long semi-ripe cuttings and insert in pots placed in gentle warmth.

Ceanothus x delileanus 'Gloire de Versailles' (Californian Lilac) Hardy deciduous shrub – in mid-summer take 7.5 cm (3 in) long semi-ripe cuttings and insert in pots placed in gentle warmth.

Ceanothus dentatus (Californian Lilac) Hardy evergreen shrub – in mid-summer take 7.5 cm (3 in) long semi-ripe cuttings and insert in pots placed in gentle warmth.

Ceanothus 'Gloire de Versailles' See *Ceanothus x delileanus* 'Gloire de Versailles'.

Ceanothus impressus (Californian Lilac) Half-hardy evergreen shrub – in mid-summer take 7.5 cm (3 in) long semi-ripe cuttings and insert in pots placed in gentle warmth.

Ceanothus rigidus (Californian Lilac) Half-hardy evergreen shrub – in mid-summer take 7.5 cm (3 in) long semi-ripe cuttings and insert in pots placed in gentle warmth.

Ceanothus thyrsiflorus (Blue Blossom, Californian Lilac) Hardy evergreen shrub – in mid-summer take 7.5 cm (3 in) long semi-ripe cuttings and insert in pots placed in gentle warmth.

Ceanothus thyrsiflorus var. repens (Blue Blossom, Californian Lilac) Hardy evergreen shrub – in mid-summer take 7.5 cm (3 in) long semi-ripe cuttings and insert in pots placed in gentle warmth.

Cedrus (Cedar) Hardy evergreen conifers – during mid- and late spring sow seeds in pots and place in a cold frame.

Celastrus orbiculatus (Climbing Bittersweet, Oriental Bittersweet, Staff Vine) Hardy deciduous climber – during autumn layer low-growing stems. Alternatively, in mid-summer take 10 cm (4 in) long half-ripe cuttings and insert in pots placed in gentle warmth.

Celosia argentea var. cristata (Cockscomb) Greenhouse annual – sow 3 mm (⅛ in) deep.

Celosia argentea var. plumosa (Prince of Wales Feather) Half-hardy annual – sow 3 mm (⅛ in) deep.

Centaurea Lift and divide herbaceous perennials in autumn or spring. Additionally, sow seeds of perennial species in spring and place in a cold frame.

Centaurea cyanus (Cornflower) Hardy annual – sow 12 mm (½ in) deep.

Centaurea moschata (Sweet Sultan) Hardy annual – sow 6 mm (¼ in) deep.

Centranthus ruber (Valerian) Hardy herbaceous perennial – sow seeds 6 mm (¼ in) deep.

Cerastium tomentosum (Snow-in-summer) Hardy herbaceous perennial – sow seeds 6 mm (¼ in) deep.

Ceratostigma plumbaginoides Shrubby perennial – in spring lift and divide congested plants.

Ceratostigma willmottianum (Chinese Plumbago) Half-hardy deciduous shrub – during mid-summer take 7.5 cm (3 in) long half-ripe heel cuttings and insert in pots placed in gentle warmth.

Cercidiphyllum japonicum (Katsura Tree) Hardy deciduous tree – in early spring sow seeds in pots placed in a cold frame.

Cercis siliquastrum (Judas Tree, Love Tree) Hardy deciduous tree or large shrub – in early and mid-spring sow seeds in pots and place in gentle warmth.

C **A–Z OF PROPAGATING PLANTS** C

Chaenomeles

Chaenomeles (Cydonia, Japanese Quince, Japonica) Hardy deciduous shrubs – in late summer layer low-growing stems. Alternatively, in mid- and late summer take 10 cm (4 in) long heel cuttings and insert in pots in gentle warmth.

Chamaecyparis (Cypress) Hardy evergreen conifers – during late spring take 10 cm (4 in) long heel cuttings and insert in pots placed in a cold frame.

Cheiranthus (Wallflower) See *Erysimum* spp.

Chelone (Turtle Head) Hardy herbaceous perennials – during autumn or spring lift and divide congested plants.

Chimonanthus praecox (Winter Sweet) Deciduous shrub – layer long, low-growing shoots in early autumn or spring. Alternatively, sow seeds in early or mid-autumn.

Chionodoxa (Glory of the Snow) Hardy bulbous plant – as soon as the foliage dies down, lift and divide congested plants. Alternatively, in late spring sow seeds in a nursery bed.

Chlorophytum comosum (Spider Plant) Tender greenhouse and house plant – during spring divide congested plants. Alternatively, peg young plantlets into compost (see page 36); sever the stems from the parent plant when rooted.

Choisya ternata (Mexican Orange Blossom) Hardy evergreen shrub – in late summer take 7.5 cm (3 in) long half-ripe cuttings and place in gentle warmth.

Chrysanthemum carinatum (Annual Chrysanthemum, Tricoloured Chrysanthemum) Hardy annual – sow 6 mm (¼ in) deep.

Chrysanthemum coccineum See *Tanacetum coccineum*.

Chrysanthemum coronarium Hardy annual – sow 6 mm (¼ in) deep.

Chrysanthemum maximum (Shasta Daisy) See *Leucanthemum maximum*.

Chrysanthemum parthenium See *Tanacetum parthenium*.

Chrysanthemum ptarmiciflorum See *Tanacetum ptarmiciflorum*.

Cimicifuga (Bugbane) Hardy herbaceous perennial – during autumn or spring lift and divide congested plants.

Cineraria cruenta See *Pericallis* x *hybrida*.

Cineraria maritima See *Senecio cineraria*.

Cissus antarctica (Kangaroo Vine) Tender greenhouse or house plant – during early or mid-spring take 7.5 cm (3 in) long cuttings and insert in pots placed in gentle warmth. Alternatively, use layering.

Cissus discolor (Begonia Vine) Tender greenhouse or house plant – in early or mid-spring take 7.5 cm (3 in) long cuttings and insert in pots placed in gentle warmth.

Cissus rhombifolia (Grape Ivy) Tender greenhouse or house plant – during early or mid-spring take 7.5 cm (3 in) long cuttings and insert in pots placed in gentle warmth. Alternatively, use layering.

Cistus (Rock Rose, Sun Rose) Sow seeds in spring. However, seedlings may vary widely. Raise hybrids from non-flowering, half-ripe, 6 cm (2½ in) long heel cuttings in early or mid-summer and place in gentle warmth.

Clarkia elegans (Clarkia) Hardy annual – sow 6 mm (¼ in) deep.

Clarkia pulchella (Clarkia) Hardy annual – sow 6 mm (¼ in) deep.

Clematis

Clematis A range of hardy and tender, evergreen and deciduous, herbaceous and woody climbers:

• **Herbaceous species** – during mid- and late spring take 7.5 cm (3 in) long basal cuttings and insert in pots in a cold frame.

• **Climbing species** – in spring layer low-growing shoots. Rooting usually takes about a year. Alternatively, in mid-summer take 10–13 cm (4–5 in) long half-ripe cuttings with two buds at the base. Insert them in pots and place in gentle warmth.

Cleome spinosa (Spider Flower) Half-hardy annual – sow 3 mm (⅛ in) deep.

Clethra Hardy deciduous and evergreen shrubs – during mid- and late summer take 7.5–10 cm (3–4 in) long heel cuttings from lateral shoots and insert in pots placed in gentle warmth. Alternatively, during autumn layer low-growing shoots.

C **A–Z OF PROPAGATING PLANTS** C

Coleus blumei See *Solenostemon scutellarioides*.

Consolida ajacis (Larkspur) Hardy annual – sow 6 mm (¼ in) deep.

Consolida ambigua See *Consolida ajacis*.

Convallaria majalis (Lily-of-the-Valley) Hardy herbaceous perennial – during autumn or early spring lift and divide congested plants.

Convolvulus tricolor Hardy annual – sow 12 mm (½ in) deep.

Cordyline fruticosa (Ti-palm) Greenhouse or house plant – vertical or horizontal cane cuttings (see page 28).

Coreopsis tinctoria (Tickseed) Hardy annual – sow 6 mm (¼ in) deep. Sometimes it is raised as a half-hardy annual – sow 3 mm (⅛ in) deep.

Coreopsis verticillata Hardy herbaceous perennial – lift and divide congested plants in autumn or spring.

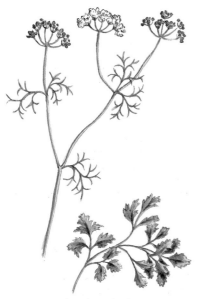

Coriandrum sativum

Coriandrum sativum (Coriander) Hardy annual – sow 6 mm (¼ in) deep.

Cornus alba (Red-barked Dogwood) Hardy, suckering shrub – in late autumn or early spring remove and replant rooted suckers. Alternatively, layer long shoots in late summer.

Cornus canadensis (Dwarf Cornel) Hardy herbaceous perennial with a creeping rootstock – lift and divide congested clumps in autumn or spring.

Cornus florida (Flowering Dogwood) Hardy deciduous shrub or small tree – sow seeds in late summer in sandy, loam-based compost in pots and place in a cold frame. Alternatively, in mid- or late summer take 7.5–10 cm (3–4 in) long half-ripe heel cuttings and insert in pots in gentle warmth.

Cornus kousa (Flowering Dogwood) Hardy deciduous shrub or small tree – sow seeds in late summer in sandy, loam-based compost in pots and place in a cold frame. Alternatively, in mid- or late summer take 7.5–10 cm (3–4 in) long half-ripe heel cuttings and insert in pots in gentle warmth.

Cornus mas (Cornelian Cherry) Hardy deciduous shrub – sow seeds in late summer in sandy, loam-based compost in pots and place in a cold frame. Alternatively, in mid- or late summer take 7.5–10 cm (3–4 in) long half-ripe heel cuttings; insert in pots in gentle warmth.

Cornus nuttallii (Mountain Dogwood) Hardy deciduous shrub or tree – sow seeds in late summer in sandy, loam-based compost in pots and place in a cold frame. Alternatively, in mid- or late summer take 7.5–10 cm (3–4 in) long half-ripe heel cuttings; insert in pots in gentle warmth.

Cornus sericea (Dogwood) Hardy, suckering shrub – in late autumn or early spring remove and replant rooted suckers. Alternatively, layer long shoots during late summer.

Cornus stolonifera See *Cornus sericea*.

Cortaderia selloana (Pampas Grass) Perennial evergreen grass – lift and divide large clumps in spring (take care to wear thick gloves).

Corylopsis Hardy deciduous shrubs or small trees – in autumn layer low-growing stems. Alternatively, in mid- or late summer take 7.5–10 cm (3–4 in) long heel cuttings and insert in pots placed in gentle warmth.

Corylus Hardy deciduous shrubs and trees – in autumn layer low-growing stems.

Cosmea See *Cosmos bipinnatus*.

Cosmos bipinnatus (Cosmea, Mexican Aster) Half-hardy annual – sow 6 mm (¼ in) deep.

Cotinus Hardy deciduous trees and shrubs – during autumn layer low-growing shoots. Alternatively, in late summer or early autumn take 10 cm (4 in) long heel cuttings from lateral shoots and insert in pots placed in a cold frame.

Cotoneaster Hardy evergreen and deciduous shrubs – in late autumn layer low-growing stems. Alternatively, in mid- and late summer take 7.5–10 cm (3–4 in) long half-ripe cuttings of deciduous species and insert in pots placed in a cold frame. In late summer and early autumn take similar cuttings of evergreen species and insert in pots placed in a cold frame.

Cotula barbata (Pincushion Plant) Half-hardy annual – sow 3 mm (⅛ in) deep.

Crambe cordifolia (Colewort) Hardy herbaceous perennial – lift and divide congested plants in spring. Alternatively, take root cuttings.

Crinum Tender bulbous plants – during early spring remove and pot up offsets and place in gentle warmth.

Crocosmia x crocosmiiflora (Montbretia) Slightly tender, cormous plant – lift and divide congested plants in early spring just before growth commences. Alternatively, in autumn sow seeds in pots placed in a cold frame.

Crocus Hardy corms – lift the corms soon after the foliage turns brown and dry the small corms in trays in a warm shed or greenhouse for a few days. During late summer or autumn replant large corms, but place small ones in a nursery bed.

Cryptomeria japonica (Japanese Cedar) Hardy evergreen conifer – during autumn take 7.5–10 cm (3–4 in) long cuttings and insert in pots placed in a cold frame.

Ctenanthe oppenheimiana 'Tricolor' (Never Never Plant) Greenhouse or house plant – divide congested roots.

Cupressus

Cupressus (True Cypress) Hardy evergreen conifers – in late summer take 7.5 cm (3 in) long cuttings from the tips of lateral shoots and insert in pots placed in a cold frame.

Cyclamen Hardy corms – during late summer or early autumn sow seeds in pots and placed in gentle warmth.

Cynoglossum amabile (Hound's Tongue) Hardy annual – sow seeds 6 mm (¼ in) deep.

Cytisus (Broom) Hardy and mainly deciduous shrubs – during mid-spring sow seeds in pots and place in a cold frame. Layer low-growing shoots in late summer. Alternatively, take 7.5 cm (3 in) long heel cuttings in mid-summer and insert in pots placed in gentle warmth.

Dahlia Half-hardy, tuberous-rooted plants. There are two groups: bedding dahlias are raised in the same way as half-hardy annuals from seeds – sow 6 mm (¼ in) deep. Border types are increased by division of tubers or by cuttings.

Daphne Evergreen and deciduous shrubs – many can be increased by layering low-growing shoots in late summer or early autumn. Alternatively, in mid- and late summer take 5–10 cm (2–4 in) long heel cuttings from non-flowering lateral shoots. Insert in pots and place in a cold frame. Increase *Daphne mezereum* from seeds.

Davidia involucrata (Dove Tree, Ghost Tree, Handkerchief Tree) Hardy deciduous tree – during mid- and late summer take 10–13 cm (4–5 in) long heel cuttings from lateral shoots and insert in pots placed in a cold frame. Alternatively, in early autumn layer low-growing shoots.

Delphinium elatum Hardy herbaceous perennial – lift and divide congested clumps in spring. Alternatively, in spring take 7.5 cm (3 in) long softwood cuttings from the bases of plants.

Deutzia Hardy deciduous shrubs – during mid- and late summer take 7.5–10 cm (3–4 in) long half-ripe cuttings and insert in pots placed in a cold frame.

Dianthus barbatus (Sweet William) Perennial usually grown as a hardy biennial – sow 6 mm (¼ in) deep.

Dianthus chinensis (Indian Pink) Biennial or short-lived perennial grown as a half-hardy annual – sow 3 mm (⅛ in) deep.

Dicentra (Bleeding Heart) Hardy herbaceous perennials – lift and divide congested plants in autumn or spring.

Dictamnus albus (Burning Bush) Hardy herbaceous perennial – sow freshly gathered seeds in a nursery bed outdoors in late summer or early autumn. In mid-autumn transfer the seedlings to their flowering positions. Alternatively, during late summer sow seeds in a nursery bed outdoors.

Dieffenbachia (Dumb Cane) Greenhouse or house plant – during late spring and early summer take stem-tip cuttings or cane cuttings. Insert in pots placed in gentle warmth. Air-layer *D. maculata*.

Digitalis purpurea (Foxglove) Hardy biennial – sow 3 mm (⅛ in) deep.

Dimorphotheca ecklonis 'Prostrata' See *Osteospermum ecklonis* var. *prostratum*.

Dipelta floribunda

Dipelta floribunda Hardy deciduous shrub – during mid- and late summer take half-ripe 7.5–10 cm (3–4 in) long cuttings and insert in pots placed in a cold frame. Alternatively, in autumn take 30 cm (12 in) long hardwood cuttings and insert in a nursery bed outdoors.

Dizygotheca elegantissima See *Schefflera elegantissima*.

Dorycnium hirsutum See *Lotus hirsutum*.

Dracaena Greenhouse and house plants – during spring take basal shoots and insert them in pots placed in gentle warmth. Alternatively, use stems as cane cuttings, or take leaf-bud cuttings.

Dryopteris Mainly perennials – in spring, sow spores (see Glossary), or divide congested plants.

A–Z OF PROPAGATING PLANTS

Echeveria Greenhouse or house plants – during spring take leaf cuttings.

Echinacea purpurea (Purple Cone Flower) Hardy herbaceous perennial – lift and divide congested plants in autumn or spring. Alternatively, raise plants by sowing seeds in a seed bed in spring.

Echium lycopsis See *Echium plantagineum*.

Echium plantagineum (Viper's Bugloss) Hardy annual – sow 6 mm (¼ in) deep.

Elaeagnus angustifolia (Oleaster) Hardy deciduous tree or shrub – during summer and into early autumn sow seeds in pots placed in a cold frame.

Elaeagnus argentea See *Elaeagnus commutata*.

Elaeagnus commutata (Silver Berry) Hardy deciduous shrub – during summer and into early autumn sow seeds in pots placed in a cold frame. This shrub produces suckers, and these can be detached in autumn and planted in a nursery bed or growing positions.

Elaeagnus x ebbingei Hardy evergreen shrub – during late summer and early autumn take 7.5–10 cm (3–4 in) long cuttings and insert in pots placed in a cold frame.

Elaeagnus macrophylla Hardy evergreen shrub – during late summer and early autumn take 7.5–10 cm (3–4 in) long cuttings and insert in pots placed in a cold frame.

Elaeagnus pungens Hardy evergreen shrub – during late summer and early autumn take 7.5–10 cm (3–4 in) long cuttings and insert in pots placed in a cold frame.

Emilia coccinea (Tassel Flower) Half-hardy annual – sow 3 mm (⅛ in) deep.

Endymion hispanicus See *Hyacinthoides hispanica*.

Enkianthus campanulatus Hardy deciduous shrub – during late summer and early autumn take 7.5 cm (3 in) long heel cuttings from lateral shoots and insert in pots placed in a cold frame.

Epimedium (Barrenwort, Bishop's Hat) Hardy, rhizomatous-rooted, semi- or evergreen perennials – lift and divide congested clumps in autumn or spring.

Epipremnum aureum (Devil's Ivy) Greenhouse or house plant – layer long stems in late spring or early summer.

Eranthis hyemalis (Winter Aconite) Hardy tuberous plant – lift and divide congested plants as the foliage begins to die down and replant them immediately.

Eremurus (Foxtail Lily) Hardy herbaceous perennials – during autumn lift and divide congested plants.

Erica (Heather, Heath) Evergreen shrubs:

• **Hardy garden species** – from mid-summer to early autumn take 2.5–5 cm (1–2 in) long young heel cuttings from sideshoots and insert in well-drained compost. Place in gentle warmth and spray regularly with clean water.

• **Greenhouse species** – in early and mid-spring take 2.5 cm (1 in) long cuttings inserted in equal parts moist peat and sharp sand and placed in gentle warmth.

Erigeron speciosus (Fleabane) Hardy herbaceous perennial – divide congested plants in autumn or spring.

Eryngium Hardy or tender herbaceous perennials – many can be increased from vertical root cuttings.

Erysimum x allionii (Siberian Wallflower) Hardy perennial that is usually grown as a biennial – sow 6 mm (¼ in) deep.

Erysimum alpinum (Alpine Wallflower, Fairy Wallflower) Hardy biennial – sow 6 mm (¼ in) deep.

Erysimum cheiri (Wallflower) Hardy perennial usually grown as a biennial – sow 6 mm (¼ in) deep.

Escallonia (garden varieties) Slightly tender evergreen shrubs – during late summer and early autumn take 7.5–10 cm (3–4 in) long heel cuttings and insert in pots placed in a cold frame. Slight bottom heat encourages rooting.

Eschscholzia californica (Californian Poppy) Hardy annual – sow 6 mm (¼ in) deep.

Eucalyptus (Gum Trees) Evergreen shrubs and trees, some fully hardy in temperate areas – during late winter or early spring sow seeds 3 mm (⅛ in) deep in finely sifted compost in pots and placed in gentle warmth. Germination is usually within 14 days, but the seeds of some species such as *E. coccifera* (Mount Wellington Peppermint), *E. niphophila* (Alpine Snow Gum) and *E. pauciflora* (Cabbage Gum) need first to be stratified in cold and wet conditions for up to eight weeks. After germination, transfer the seedlings to individual pots as soon as the first pair of seed leaves are formed.

Eucryphia

Eucryphia Deciduous, evergreen or partially evergreen trees and shrubs – during late summer or early autumn take 7.5–10 cm (3–4 in) long half-ripe heel cuttings from the current season's growth and insert in pots placed in gentle warmth.

Euonymus alatus Hardy deciduous shrub – during autumn sow seeds in pots and place in a cold frame. Alternatively, in late summer take 7.5 cm (3 in) long heel cuttings and insert in pots also placed in a cold frame.

Euonymus europaeus (Common Spindle Tree) Hardy deciduous shrub or small tree – during autumn layer low-growing stems. Alternatively, in late summer take 7.5 cm (3 in) long heel cuttings and insert in pots placed in a cold frame.

Euonymus fortunei Hardy evergreen shrub – in autumn layer low-growing stems. Alternatively, in late summer or early autumn take 7.5 cm (3 in) long heel cuttings and insert in pots placed in a cold frame. Congested plants can also be divided in spring.

Euonymus japonicus Hardy evergreen shrub – in autumn layer low-growing stems. Alternatively, in late summer or early autumn take 7.5 cm (3 in) long heel cuttings and insert in pots placed in a cold frame.

Euphorbia characias Hardy herbaceous perennial – during autumn or spring lift and divide congested plants.

Euphorbia marginata (Snow on the Mountain) Hardy annual – sow 6 mm (¼ in) deep.

Euphorbia milii (Crown of Thorns) Semi-succulent greenhouse or house plant – during mid-summer take 7.5 cm (3 in) long cuttings and insert (first allow to dry for a couple of days) in pots placed in gentle warmth.

Euphorbia polychroma Hardy evergreen sub-shrubby perennial – during autumn or spring lift and divide congested plants.

Euphorbia pulcherrima (Poinsettia) Greenhouse or house plant – during spring take 7.5–10 cm (3–4 in) long cuttings from plants earlier cut back. Insert them in pots placed in gentle warmth.

Euphorbia splendens See *Euphorbia milii.*

Fagus sylvatica (Beech) Hardy deciduous tree – during autumn sow seeds outdoors in a seed bed. When the seedlings are large enough to handle, transfer them to a nursery bed or their permanent positions.

Fallopia baldschuanica (Mile-a-minute-Vine, Russian Vine) Hardy deciduous climber – during mid- and late summer take 7.5–10 cm (3–4 in) long half-ripe cuttings and insert in pots placed in a cold frame.

x Fatshedera lizei (Ivy Tree) Hardy evergreen shrub – during mid- and late summer take 10 cm (4 in) long tip and stem cuttings. Insert in pots and place in a cold frame.

Fatsia japonica

Fatsia japonica (False Castor Oil Plant) Hardy or slightly tender evergreen shrub – during spring detach sucker-like shoots from around the base of a plant and pot up in individual pots placed in a cold frame.

Felicia bergeriana (Kingfisher Daisy) Half-hardy annual – sow 3 mm (⅛ in) deep.

Festuca Hardy perennial grasses – during autumn or spring lift and divide congested plants.

Feverfew See *Tanacetum parthenium.*

Ficus benjamina (Weeping Fig) Greenhouse or house plant – during spring and early summer take 5–7.5 cm (2–3 in) long cuttings from lateral shoots and insert in pots placed in gentle warmth.

Ficus deltoidea See *Ficus diversifolia.*

Ficus diversifolia (Mistletoe Fig) Greenhouse or house plant – during spring and early summer take 5–7.5 cm (2–3 in) long cuttings from lateral shoots and insert in pots placed in gentle warmth.

Ficus elastica (Rubber Plant) Greenhouse or house plant – during late spring and early summer take 10–15 cm (4–6 in) long cuttings and insert in pots placed in gentle warmth. Alternatively, during late spring and early summer take leaf-bud cuttings. Also, from late spring to mid-summer air-layer plants.

Ficus lyrata (Fiddle-back Fig) Greenhouse or house plant – during late spring and early summer take 10–15 cm (4–6 in) long cuttings and insert in pots placed in gentle warmth. Alternatively, from late spring to mid-summer air-layer plants.

Ficus pumila (Creeping Fig) Greenhouse or house plant – during spring and early summer take 5–7.5 cm (2–3 in) long cuttings from lateral shoots and insert in pots placed in gentle warmth.

Ficus radicans (Trailing Fig) Greenhouse or house plant – during spring and early summer take 5–7.5 cm (2–3 in) long cuttings from lateral shoots and insert in pots placed in gentle warmth.

Filipendula purpurea (Meadowsweet) Hardy herbaceous perennial – lift and divide congested plants in autumn or early spring.

Foeniculum vulgare (Fennel) Hardy herbaceous perennial – sow 6 mm (¼ in) deep.

Forsythia (Golden Bells) Hardy deciduous shrubs – in early autumn take 25 cm (10 in) long hardwood cuttings and insert 10–15 cm (4–6 in) deep in a nursery bed outdoors. Form a narrow trench and spread coarse sand in its base.

Fothergilla Hardy deciduous shrubs – in early autumn layer low-growing stems.

Fremontia californica See *Fremontodendron californicum.*

Fremontodendron californicum Slightly tender deciduous or semi-evergreen wall-shrub – during early and mid-spring sow seeds 3 mm (⅛ in) deep in pots placed in gentle warmth.

Fuchsia (Lady's Eardrops) Tender greenhouse and summer-bedding shrubs – in spring take 7.5 cm (3 in) long cuttings from the tips of shoots and insert in pots placed in gentle warmth.

Fuchsia magellanica

Fuchsia magellanica (Hardy Fuchsia, Lady's Eardrops) Slightly tender deciduous shrub – lift and divide congested clumps in spring.

Gaillardia aristata (Blanket Flower) Hardy herbaceous perennial – lift and divide congested clumps in spring.

Gaillardia pulchella (Blanket Flower) Half-hardy annual – sow 3 mm (⅛ in) deep.

Galanthus nivalis (Common Snowdrop) Hardy bulb – lift and divide congested clumps as soon as they finish flowering. Replant them immediately so that the bulbs do not become dry.

Garrya elliptica Hardy evergreen shrub – during early autumn layer low-growing stems. Alternatively, during late summer and early autumn take 7.5–10 cm (3–4 in) long half-ripe heel cuttings and insert in pots placed in a cold frame.

Gaultheria mucronata Hardy evergreen shrub – increase the species from seeds sown in autumn in pots in a cold frame. Named varieties have to be raised from 5 cm (2 in) long cuttings taken in early autumn and inserted in pots in a cold frame.

Gazania x hybrida Half-hardy annual – sow 3–6 mm (⅛– ¼ in) deep.

Genista (Broom) Hardy deciduous shrubs – in mid- or late summer take 7.5 cm (3 in) long heel cutting from sideshoots of the current season's growth and insert in pots placed in a cold frame. Alternatively, in spring sow seeds in pots of sandy soil and place in a cold frame.

Geranium (Crane's-bill) Hardy herbaceous perennial – lift and divide congested plants in autumn or spring.

Gerbera jamesonii (Barberton Daisy, Transvaal Daisy) Tender perennial – just press seeds on the surface of the compost.

Geum (Avens) Hardy herbaceous perennials – lift and divide congested plants in spring.

Ginkgo biloba (Maidenhair Tree) Hardy deciduous conifer – during early and mid-autumn sow seeds in pots placed in a cold frame. Sow as soon as the seeds are ripe.

Gladiolus Tender cormous plant – during late spring plant young cormlets removed from plants that were lifted late during the previous year and allowed to become dry. These are usually planted in a nursery bed for later (after 2–3 years) planting in their flowering positions.

***Glechoma hederacea* 'Variegata'** (Variegated Ground Ivy) Hardy perennial – during spring lift and divide congested plants.

Glyceria maxima* var. *variegata (Variegated Reed Sweetgrass) Hardy herbaceous aquatic – during spring lift and divide congested clumps.

Godetia Hardy annual – sow 6 mm (¼ in) deep.

Gomphrena globosa (Batchelor's Button, Globe Amaranth) Half-hardy annual – sow 6 mm (¼ in) deep.

Griselinia littoralis Slightly tender evergreen shrub – during late summer and early autumn take 7.5–10 cm (3–4 in) long cuttings from sideshoots and insert in pots placed in a cold frame.

Gunnera manicata Slightly tender herbaceous perennial – in mid- and late spring cut away small crowns that have started to develop roots from around the main plant. Put them into pots, keep moist and in a shady area until established.

Gypsophila elegans (Baby's Breath) Hardy annual – sow 6 mm (¼ in) deep.

Gypsophila paniculata (Baby's Breath) Hardy herbaceous perennial – during mid- and late spring take 7.5 cm (3 in) long cuttings from around the plant's base. Insert them in pots of equal parts moist peat and sharp sand and place in a cold frame.

Hakonechloa macra Hardy perennial grass – lift and divide congested clumps in spring.

Hamamelis

Hamamelis (Witch Hazel) Hardy deciduous shrubs or small trees – layer low-growing stems in late summer. Alternatively, take 10 cm (4 in) long cuttings from the current season's shoots in late summer and insert in pots in a cold frame.

Hebe (Shrubby Veronica) Hardy evergreen shrubs – in mid- and late summer take 5–10 cm (2–4 in) long cuttings from non-flowering shoots and insert in pots placed in a cold frame.

Hedera (Ivies) Hardy evergreen climbers or house plants; see below for individual varieties. House plants may also be layered (see page 34).

Hedera canariensis 'Gloire de Marengo' (Variegated Canary Island Ivy) Hardy evergreen climber – during mid-summer take 7.5–10 cm (3–4 in) long cuttings and insert in pots placed in gentle warmth. Take the cuttings from long shoots of the current season's growth.

Hedera canariensis 'Variegata' See *Hedera canariensis* 'Gloire de Marengo'.

Hedera colchica 'Dentata Variegata' (Variegated Persian Ivy) Hardy evergreen climber – during mid-summer take 7.5–10 cm (3–4 in) long cuttings and insert in pots placed in gentle warmth. If the plant is to be grown as a climber, take the cuttings from long shoots of the current season's growth. If it is to be grown as a ground-cover plant, take the cuttings from older wood.

Hedera colchica 'Paddy's Pride' See Hedera colchica 'Sulphur Heart'.

Hedera colchica 'Sulphur Heart' Hardy evergreen climber – during mid-summer take 7.5–10 cm (3–4 in) long cuttings and insert in pots placed in gentle warmth. If the plant is to be grown as a climber, take the cuttings from long shoots of the current season's growth. If it is to be grown as a ground-cover plant, take the cuttings from older wood.

Hedera colchica 'Variegata' See *Hedera colchica* 'Dentata Variegata'.

Hedera helix 'Glacier' Hardy small-leaved evergreen climber – during mid-summer take 7.5 cm (3 in) long cuttings from the current season's growth and insert in pots placed in gentle warmth.

Hedera helix 'Goldheart'

Hedera helix 'Goldheart' Hardy small-leaved evergreen climber – during mid-summer take 7.5 cm (3 in) long cuttings from the current season's growth and insert in pots placed in gentle warmth.

Helenium autumnale (Sneezewort) Hardy herbaceous perennial – lift and divide congested plants in autumn or spring.

Helianthemum (Rock Rose, Sun Rose) Hardy low-growing evergreen shrubs – from early to late summer take 5–7.5 cm (2–3 in) long heel cuttings from non-flowering shoots and insert in pots placed in a cold frame.

Helianthus Hardy herbaceous perennials – during autumn or spring lift and divide congested plants.

Helianthus annuus (Sunflower) Hardy annual – sow 12 mm (½ in) deep.

Helichrysum angustifolia See *Helichrysum italicum*.

Helichrysum bracteatum See *Xerochrysum bracteatum*.

Helichrysum italicum (Curry Plant, White-leaf Everlasting) Half-hardy sub-shrubby perennial – during mid-summer take 7.5 cm (3 in) long cuttings from the current season's growth and insert in pots placed in a cold frame.

Helichrysum petiolare (Licorice Plant) Tender shrubby perennial – during mid- to late summer take 7.5 cm (3 in) long cuttings from side shoots and insert in pots placed in gentle warmth.

Heliotropium arborescens (Cherry Pie, Heliotrope) Half-hardy perennial usually grown as a half-hardy annual – sow 6 mm (¼ in) deep.

Helleborus Hardy evergreen and deciduous perennials – sow seeds (when ripe) in early or mid-summer in pots and place in a cold frame.

Helleborus niger (Christmas Rose) Hardy perennial with evergreen leaves – lift and divide congested plants in spring after the flowers fade.

Helleborus orientalis (Lenten Rose) Hardy perennial with evergreen leaves – lift and divide congested plants in spring after the flowers fade.

Hemerocallis (Day Lily) Hardy herbaceous perennials – lift and divide congested plants in autumn or spring.

Heptapleurum arboricola See *Schefflera arboricola*.

Hesperis matronalis (Sweet Rocket) Hardy perennial – sow 6 mm (¼ in) deep.

Heuchera sanguinea (Coral Flower) Hardy herbaceous perennial – during autumn and spring lift and divide congested plants.

Hibiscus syriacus (Shrubby Mallow) Hardy deciduous shrub – during mid-summer take 7.5–10 cm (3–4 in) long half-ripe heel cuttings from non-flowering shoots and insert in pots placed in gentle warmth.

Hibiscus trionum (Flower-of-an-hour) Hardy annual – sow 6 mm (¼ in) deep.

Hosta (Plantain Lily) Hardy herbaceous perennials – lift and divide congested plants in early or mid-spring just as growth begins.

***Humulus lupulus* 'Aureus'** (Golden-leaved Hop, Yellow European Hop) Hardy herbaceous perennial – during late autumn or spring lift and divide congested plants.

Hyacinthoides hispanica (Bluebell, Spanish Bluebell) Hardy bulb – immediately the flowers fade, lift and divide congested clumps. Alternatively, scatter ripe seeds on the soil's surface and lightly cover with friable soil.

Hydrangea anomala* subsp. *petiolaris (Japanese Climbing Hydrangea) Hardy deciduous climber – during mid-summer take 7.5 cm (3 in) long cuttings from the current season's growth and insert in pots placed in a cold frame.

Hydrangea arborescens (Hills of Snow) Hardy deciduous shrub – during mid- and late summer take 10–15 cm (4–6 in) long cuttings from non-flowering shoots of the current season's growth. Insert them in pots and place in gentle warmth.

Hydrangea aspera Hardy deciduous shrub – during mid- and late summer take 10–13 cm (4–5 in) long cuttings from non-flowering shoots of the current season's growth. Insert them in pots and place in gentle warmth.

Hydrangea macrophylla

Hydrangea macrophylla (Common Hydrangea, French Hydrangea) Hardy deciduous shrub – during mid- and late summer take 10–13 cm (4–5 in) long cuttings from non-flowering shoots of the current season's growth. Insert them in pots and place in gentle warmth.

Hydrangea paniculata Hardy deciduous shrub – during mid- and late summer take 10–13 cm (4–5 in) long cuttings from non-flowering shoots of the current season's growth. Insert them in pots and place in gentle warmth.

Hydrangea petiolaris See *Hydrangea anomala* subsp. *petiolaris*.

Hydrangea quercifolia Hardy deciduous shrub – during mid- and late summer take 10–15 cm (4–6 in) long cuttings from non-flowering shoots of the current season's growth. Insert them in pots and place in gentle warmth.

Hydrangea scandens See *Hydrangea anomala* subsp. *petiolaris*.

***Hypericum* 'Hidcote'** (Rose of Sharon, St John's Wort) Almost evergreen hardy shrub – in mid-summer take 10–13 cm (4–5 in) long heel cuttings from the current season's shoots and insert in pots placed in a cold frame.

Hypericum olympicum Hardy evergreen shrub – in early summer take 5 cm (2 in) long basal cuttings from the current season's shoots and insert in pots placed in a cold frame.

***Hypericum patulum* 'Hidcote'** See *Hypericum* 'Hidcote'.

Hyssopus officinalis (Hyssop) Hardy perennial – sow 6 mm (¼ in) deep.

Iberis umbellata (Candytuft) Hardy annual – sow 6 mm (¼ in) deep.

Ilex x altaclerensis Hardy evergreen shrub or small tree – in late summer take 5–7.5 cm (2–3 in) long heel cuttings and insert in pots placed in a cold frame. Alternatively, layer low-growing shoots in autumn.

Ilex aquifolium (Common Holly, English Holly) Hardy evergreen shrub or small tree – in late summer take 5–7.5 cm (2–3 in) long heel cuttings and insert in pots placed in a cold frame. Alternatively, layer low-growing shoots in autumn.

Impatiens balsamina (Balsam, Touch-me-not) Half-hardy annual – sow 6 mm (¼ in) deep.

Impatiens sultani See *Impatiens walleriana*.

Impatiens walleriana (Busy Lizzie) Greenhouse perennial usually grown as a half-hardy annual – sow 3 mm (⅛ in) deep. You can also root softwood cuttings in water (see page 20).

Incarvillea Hardy herbaceous perennials – lift and divide congested plants in autumn. Additionally, in spring sow seeds in a seed bed outdoors.

Ionopsidium acaule (Violet Cress) Hardy annual – sow 6 mm (¼ in) deep.

Ipheion uniflorum (Spring Starflower) Hardy bulb – as soon as the foliage dies down, lift and divide congested clumps.

Iris cristata Crested type – lift and divide congested rhizomes after the flowers fade, in late spring.

Iris danfordiae Bulbous type – lift and divide congested bulbs after the foliage has died down.

Iris ensata Beardless iris (Laevigatae) – lift congested clumps and divide rhizomes immediately after flowering, or at any time when growth is active.

Iris 'Florentina' (Florentine Iris, Orris Root) Intermediate bearded iris – see *Iris germanica* for propagation.

Iris foetidissima (Gladwyn, Stinking Iris) Beardless iris – lift and divide congested rhizomes in autumn. Can also be increased by seed.

Iris germanica

Iris germanica (Purple Flag Iris) Intermediate bearded iris – lift and divide congested rhizomes after flowering, selecting pieces from around the outside and ensuring each piece has one or two fans of leaves.

Iris histrioides Bulbous type – see *Iris danfordiae* for propagation.

Iris kaempferi See *Iris ensata*.

Iris laevigata Beardless iris (Laevigatae) – see *Iris ensata* for propagation.

Iris pallida Tall bearded iris – see *Iris germanica* for propagation.

Iris pseudacorus (Yellow Flag Iris) Beardless iris (Laevigatae) – see *Iris ensata* for propagation.

Iris pumila Dwarf bearded iris – see *Iris germanica* for propagation.

Iris reticulata Bulbous type – see *Iris danfordiae* for propagation.

Iris sibirica (Siberian Iris) Beardless iris (Sibiricae) – lift and divide congested clumps after the foliage dies down in late autumn or in spring as growth begins. Replant the rhizomes 2.5 cm (1 in) deep.

Jasminum humile 'Revolutum' Hardy, non-twining evergreen shrub sometimes trained against a wall – during autumn layer low-growing stems. Alternatively, during late summer take 7.5–10 cm (3–4 in) long half-ripe cuttings and insert in pots placed in gentle warmth.

Jasminum mesnyi (Primrose Jasmine) Slightly tender evergreen climber – during autumn layer low-growing stems. Alternatively, during late summer take 7.5–10 cm (3–4 in) long half-ripe heel cuttings and insert in pots placed in gentle warmth.

Jasminum nudiflorum (Winter-flowering Jasmine) Hardy deciduous wall shrub – during autumn layer low-growing stems.

Jasminum officinale (Common White Jasmine, Poet's Jessamine) Hardy deciduous climber – during autumn layer low-growing stems. Alternatively, during late summer take 7.5–10 cm (3–4 in) long half-ripe heel cuttings and insert in pots placed in gentle warmth.

Jasminum polyanthum (Pink Jasmine) Slightly tender climber often grown in temperate climates in a greenhouse or as a house plant – during autumn layer low-growing stems. Alternatively, during late summer take 7.5–10 cm (3–4 in) long half-ripe heel cuttings; insert in pots in gentle warmth.

Jasminum primulinum See *Jasminum mesnyi*.

Jasminum revolutum See *Jasminum humile 'Revolutum'*.

Justicia brandegeeana (Shrimp Plant) Tender greenhouse or house plant – during spring take 5–7.5 cm (2–3 in) long half-ripe stem cuttings and insert in pots placed in gentle warmth.

Kalanchoe daigremontiana (Mexican Hat Plant) Greenhouse or house plant – remove and root plantlets (see page 36).

Kalanchoe delagoensis (Chandelier Plant) Greenhouse or house plant – remove and root plantlets (see page 37).

Kalmia angustifolia (Sheep Laurel) Hardy evergreen shrub – during late summer and early autumn layer low-growing stems. Alternatively, in late summer take 10–13 cm (4–5 in) long half-ripe cuttings from the current season's shoots and insert in pots placed in a cold frame.

Kalmia latifolia (Calico Bush, Mountain Laurel) Hardy evergreen shrub – during late summer and early autumn layer low-growing stems. Alternatively, in late summer take 10–13 cm (4–5 in) long half-ripe cuttings from the current season's shoots; insert in pots in a cold frame.

Kerria japonica (Jew's Mallow) Hardy deciduous shrub – during late summer and early autumn take 10–13 cm (4–5 in) long cuttings from the current season's growth and insert in pots placed in a cold frame.

K   **A–Z OF PROPAGATING PLANTS**   **L**

Kerria japonica 'Pleniflora' (Bachelor's Buttons) Hardy deciduous shrub – during late summer and early autumn take 10–13 cm (4–5 in) long cuttings from the current season's growth and insert in pots placed in a cold frame.

Kniphofia (Poker Plant) Hardy herbaceous perennials – in early spring lift and divide congested plants. Take care not to damage the crowns.

Kochia scoparia 'Trichophylla' See *Bassia scoparia* f. *trichophylla*.

Kolkwitzia amabilis

Kolkwitzia amabilis (Beauty Bush) Hardy deciduous shrub – during mid-summer take 10–13 cm (4–5 in) long cuttings from the current season's growth and insert in pots placed in a cold frame.

Laburnum (Golden Chain Tree, Golden Rain Tree) Hardy deciduous trees – in autumn sow seeds in pots placed in a cold frame.

Laburnum x watereri 'Vossii' (Golden Chain Tree, Golden Rain Tree) Hardy deciduous tree – this hybrid does not come true when raised from seeds. Therefore, it is increased in late winter by grafting the species on to a rootstock.

Larix decidua (European Larch) Hardy deciduous conifer – during spring sow seeds directly into a nursery bed outdoors.

Lathyrus latifolius (Everlasting Sweet Pea) Hardy perennial climber – sow seeds 12 mm (½ in) deep in flowering positions in early and mid-spring.

Lathyrus odoratus (Sweet Pea) Hardy annual – sow 12 mm (½ in) deep in flowering positions in spring. Alternatively, sow seeds 12 mm (½ in) deep in seed-trays (flats) in a heated greenhouse in late winter.

Laurus nobilis (Bay, Bay Laurel, Sweet Bay) Hardy evergreen shrub – during mid- and late summer take 10 cm (4 in) long heel cuttings from sideshoots and insert in pots placed in a cold frame.

Lavandula angustifolia (Lavender, Old English Lavender) Hardy evergreen shrub – during mid- and late summer take 7.5–10 cm (3–4 in) long cuttings from non-flowering shoots; insert in pots in a cold frame.

Lavandula vera (Dutch Lavender) Hardy evergreen shrub – during mid-summer take 7.5 cm (3 in) long cuttings from non-flowering shoots and insert in pots in a cold frame.

Lavatera arborea 'Rosea' See *Lavatera* x *clementii* 'Rosea'.

Lavatera x clementii 'Rosea' (Tree Lavatera) Soft-stemmed shrub – in mid- and late summer take 7.5–10 cm (3–4 in) long cuttings from non-flowering shoots and insert in pots placed in a cold frame.

Lavatera olbia 'Rosea' See *Lavatera* x *clementii* 'Rosea'.

Lavatera trimestris (Annual Mallow) Hardy annual – sow 12 mm (½ in) deep.

Leucanthemum maximum (Shasta Daisy) Herbaceous perennial – sow 6 mm (¼ in) deep. Alternatively, during autumn or spring lift and divide congested plants.

Leucojum (Snowflake) Hardy bulbs – where clumps become congested, carefully lift them as soon as their leaves die down. Divide them and replant immediately.

Levisticum officinale (Lovage) Hardy perennial – sow seeds 6 mm (¼ in) deep in a seed bed in spring.

Liatris (Blazing Star, Gayfeather) Hardy tuberous-rooted herbaceous perennial – lift and divide congested plants in spring.

Libocedrus decurrens See *Calocedrus decurrens*.

Ligularia Hardy herbaceous perennials – in spring lift and divide congested plants.

Ligustrum japonicum (Japanese Privet) Hardy evergreen shrub – in autumn take 13–15 cm (5–6 in) long hardwood cuttings and insert in a cold frame.

Ligustrum ovalifolium (Common Privet) Hardy evergreen shrub (In severe winters it sometimes becomes semi-evergreen) – in autumn take 25–30 cm (10–12 in) long hardwood cuttings and insert in soil in a sheltered nursery bed.

Lilium (Lily) Hardy bulbs – during autumn or spring carefully lift and divide congested clumps.

Limnanthes douglasii

Limnanthes douglasii (Poached Egg Plant) Hardy annual – sow 3 mm (⅛ in) deep.

Limonium latifolium (Sea Lavender) Hardy perennial with a woody rootstock and stems. It resents root disturbance, so sow seeds 6 mm (¼ in) deep in pots and place in a cold frame in late spring or early summer.

Limonium sinuatum (Sea Lavender) Hardy perennial usually grown as a half-hardy annual – sow 6 mm (¼ in) deep.

Linaria maroccana (Toadflax) Hardy annual – sow 3 mm (⅛ in) deep.

Linum arboreum Shrubby perennial – during spring take 5 cm (2 in) long basal cuttings and insert in pots placed in a cold frame.

Linum flavum (Garden Flax) Hardy sub-shrubby perennial – during spring take 5 cm (2 in) long basal cuttings and insert in pots placed in a cold frame. Alternatively, during spring sow seeds in pots placed in a cold frame.

Linum grandiflorum (Flax) Hardy annual – sow 6 mm (¼ in) deep.

***Linum grandiflorum* 'Rubrum'** (Scarlet Flax) Hardy annual – sow 6 mm (¼ in) deep.

Linum narbonensis Hardy perennial – during spring take 5 cm (2 in) long basal cuttings and insert in pots placed in a cold frame.

Linum perenne (Perennial Flax) Hardy perennial – during spring take 5 cm (2 in) long basal cuttings and insert in pots placed in a cold frame. Alternatively, during spring sow seeds in pots placed in a cold frame.

Linum usitatissimum (Common Flax) Hardy annual – sow seeds 6 mm (¼ in) deep.

Liquidambar styraciflua (American Sweet Gum, Sweet Gum) Hardy deciduous tree – during spring layer low-growing stems. Alternatively, in mid-autumn sow seeds in pots placed in a cold frame.

Liriodendron tulipifera (Tulip Tree) Hardy deciduous tree – during spring layer low-growing stems. Alternatively, in autumn sow seeds in pots placed in a cold frame.

Lithodora diffusa (Gromwell) Hardy shrub-like perennial – during mid-summer take 5–6 cm (2–2½ in) long heel cuttings from lateral shoots and insert in pots placed in a cold frame.

Lithospermum diffusum See *Lithodora diffusa*.

Lobelia erinus (Edging Lobelia, Trailing Lobelia) Half-hardy perennial usually grown as a half-hardy annual – sow thinly and lightly press seeds into the compost.

Lobularia maritima (Sweet Alyssum) Hardy annual – sow 6 mm (¼ in) deep in flowering positions. Alternatively, raise as a half-hardy annual and sow 6 mm (¼ in) deep in gentle warmth in late winter or early spring.

Lonicera caprifolium (Goat-leaf Honeysuckle) Hardy deciduous climber – during mid- and late summer take 10 cm (4 in) long cuttings and insert in pots placed in a cold frame. Alternatively, layer low-growing shoots in late summer or autumn.

Lonicera fragrantissima Hardy partially evergreen shrub – during mid- and late summer take 10 cm (4 in) long cuttings and insert in pots placed in a cold frame. Alternatively, in autumn take 23 cm (9 in) long hardwood cuttings and insert in well-drained soil in a nursery bed.

Lonicera japonica (Japanese Honeysuckle) Hardy deciduous climber – during mid- and late summer take 10 cm (4 in) long cuttings and insert in pots placed in a cold frame. Alternatively, layer low-growing shoots in late summer or autumn.

Lonicera nitida (Chinese Honeysuckle) Hardy evergreen shrub – during mid- and late summer take 10 cm (4 in) long cuttings and insert in pots placed in a cold frame. Alternatively, in autumn take 23 cm (9 in) long hardwood cuttings and insert in well-drained soil in a nursery bed.

***Lonicera nitida* 'Baggeson's Gold'** (Yellow-leaved Chinese Honeysuckle) Hardy evergreen shrub – during mid- and late summer take 10 cm (4 in) long cuttings and insert in pots placed in a cold frame.

***Lonicera periclymenum* 'Belgica'** (Early Dutch Honeysuckle) Hardy deciduous climber – during mid- and late summer take 10 cm (4 in) long cuttings and insert in pots placed in a cold frame. Alternatively, layer low-growing shoots in late summer or autumn.

***Lonicera periclymenum* 'Serotina'** (Late Dutch Honeysuckle) Hardy deciduous climber – during mid- and late summer take 10 cm (4 in) long cuttings and insert in pots placed in a cold frame. Alternatively, layer low-growing shoots in autumn.

Lonicera standishii Hardy deciduous shrub – during mid- and late summer take 10 cm (4 in) long cuttings and insert in pots placed in a cold frame. Alternatively, in autumn take 23 cm (9 in) long hardwood cuttings and insert in well-drained soil in a nursery bed.

Lonicera tragophylla (Chinese Woodbine) Hardy deciduous climber – during mid- and late summer take 10 cm (4 in) long cuttings and insert in pots placed in a cold frame. Alternatively, layer low-growing shoots in late summer or autumn.

Lotus hirsutus (Hairy Canary Clover) Hardy semi-herbaceous woody-based dwarf shrub – during spring sow seeds in pots of sandy compost placed in a cold frame.

Lunaria annua (Honesty) Hardy biennial – sow 12 mm (½ in) deep.

Lupinus arboreus

Lupinus arboreus (Tree Lupin) Short-lived shrubby perennial – take half-ripe cuttings in early summer and place in pots in a cold frame.

Lupinus polyphyllus Hardy herbaceous perennial – sow 12 mm (½ in) deep in late spring and early summer in pots placed in a cold frame. However, named varieties need to be raised in late spring from 7.5–10 cm (3–4 in) long softwood cuttings. Preferably, a piece of the rootstock should be attached. Insert in pots of sandy soil; place in a cold frame.

Lychnis chalcedonica (Jerusalem Cross, Maltese Cross) Hardy herbaceous perennial – during spring lift and divide congested plants.

Lychnis viscaria (Annual Campion) Hardy annual – sow 6 mm (¼ in) deep.

Lysichiton (Skunk Cabbage) Hardy herbaceous perennial – during spring remove young plants from around congested clumps and pot up into individual pots. Keep moist and shaded until established.

Lysimachia (Loosestrife) Hardy herbaceous perennials – lift and divide congested plants in autumn or spring.

Lysimachia nummularia (Creeping Jenny, Moneywort) During autumn or spring lift and divide congested plants. Alternatively, in spring cut stems into 7.5–10 cm (3–4 in) long sections and insert where plants are to grow.

Lythrum salicaria (Purple Loosestrife) Hardy herbaceous perennial – during autumn or spring lift and divide congested plants.

Macleaya (Plume Poppy) Hardy herbaceous perennial – during autumn or spring lift and divide congested plants.

Magnolia Hardy evergreen and deciduous trees and shrubs – during spring layer low-growing stems. Rooting takes about two years. Alternatively, in mid-summer take 10 cm (4 in) long half-ripe heel cuttings and insert in sandy compost in pots placed in a cold frame. Placing in gentle warmth assists in the development of roots. Another way to increase magnolias is by sowing seeds in pots in autumn and placing them in a cold frame.

Mahonia Hardy evergreen shrubs – in late summer sow seeds of ground-cover species in pots placed in a cold frame. Alternatively, take 7.5–10 cm (3–4 in) long tip cuttings from sideshoots in mid-summer; insert them in equal parts moist peat and sharp sand and place in gentle warmth.

Malcolmia maritima (Virginia Stock) Hardy annual – sow 6 mm (¼ in) deep.

Malope trifida Hardy annual – sow 6 mm (¼ in) deep.

Malus

Malus – All hybrids and varieties need to be budded onto selected rootstocks.

Maranta Greenhouse or house plants – divide congested plants.

Matthiola bicornis (Night-scented Stock) Hardy annual – sow seeds 6 mm (¼ in) deep.

Matthiola incana (Stock) There are several well-known forms (treat as indicated below):

• **Ten-week Stock:** hardy annual – sow 6 mm (¼ in) deep.

• **Perpetual-flowering Stock:** hardy annual – sow 6 mm (¼ in) deep.

• **Brompton Stock:** hardy biennial – sow 6 mm (¼ in) deep.

• **East Lothian Stock:** hardy annual or hardy biennial – sow 6 mm (¼ in) deep.

Meconopsis betonicifolia (Blue Poppy, Himalayan Blue Poppy) Short-lived hardy perennial – sow 3 mm (⅛ in) deep in pots in mid-winter; leave outside until late winter and then take into gentle warmth.

Meconopsis cambrica (Welsh Poppy) Short-lived hardy perennial – sow 6 mm (¼ in) deep in a seed bed outdoors during late spring and early summer.

Melissa officinalis (Balm) Hardy herbaceous perennial – during autumn or spring lift and divide congested plants. Alternatively, during mid- and late spring sow seeds in a seed bed outdoors.

Mentha (Mint) Hardy herbaceous perennials – during early spring lift and divide congested clumps. Alternatively, in late spring or early summer take 7.5–10 cm (3–4 in) long basal cuttings and insert in pots placed in a cold frame.

Mimulus (Monkey Flower) Half-hardy annual – sow thinly and lightly press seeds into the compost.

Mirabilis jalapa (Marvel of Peru) Hardy perennial usually grown as a half-hardy annual – sow 6 mm (¼ in) deep.

Miscanthus Hardy perennial grasses – in spring lift and divide congested plants.

Molucella laevis (Bells of Ireland) Half-hardy annual – sow 6 mm (¼ in) deep.

Monarda didyma

Monarda didyma (Bee Balm, Oswego Tea, Sweet Bergamot) Herbaceous perennial – during spring lift and divide congested plants.

Monstera deliciosa (Swiss Cheese Plant) Greenhouse or house plant – air-layer from late spring to mid-summer.

Montbretia crocosmiiflora See *Crocosmia* x *crocosmiiflora*.

Muscari armeniacum (Grape Hyacinth) Hardy bulb – lift and divide congested plants as soon as the leaves turn yellow. Replant the bulbs immediately to prevent them becoming dry.

Myosotis sylvatica (Forget-me-not) Hardy biennial – sow 6 mm (¼ in) deep.

Myrrhis odorata (Sweet Cicely) Hardy herbaceous perennial – in spring divide congested plants. Alternatively, in mid-spring sow seeds in growing positions.

Narcissus (Daffodil) Hardy bulbs – lift and divide congested bulbs as soon as the foliage dies down. Flowering-sized bulbs can be replanted in autumn directly in their flowering positions, while small ones are planted in a nursery bed.

Nemesia strumosa Half-hardy annual – sow 3 mm (⅛ in) deep.

Nemophila menziesii (Baby Blue Eyes) Hardy annual – sow seeds 6 mm (¼ in) deep.

Nepeta x faassenii (Catmint) Hardy herbaceous perennial – during spring lift and divide congested plants.

Nephrolepis Greenhouse and house plants – when large enough, detach and repot young plants and place in gentle warmth.

Nicandra physalodes (Apple of Peru, Shoo Fly Plant) Hardy annual – sow 3 mm (⅛ in) deep.

Nicotiana alata (Flowering Tobacco Plant) Half-hardy annual – sow 3 mm (⅛ in) deep.

Nigella damascena (Love-in-a-mist) Hardy annual – sow 6 mm (¼ in) deep.

Nuphar lutea (Brandy Bottle, Yellow Water Lily) Hardy aquatic – during late spring or early summer lift and divide congested clumps.

Nymphaea (Waterlilies) Hardy aquatics – during early and mid-spring lift and divide congested plants when the pond is drained. Use a sharp knife and replant into separate containers.

Ocimum basilicum (Sweet Basil) Half-hardy annual – during spring sow seeds 6 mm (¼ in) deep in pots placed in gentle warmth. Alternatively, in late spring sow seeds in their growing positions.

Oenothera biennis (Common Evening Primrose, German Rampion) Hardy biennial – sow 3–6 mm (⅛– ¼ in) deep. Produces many self-sown seedlings.

Oenothera trichocalyx (Evening Primrose) Hardy biennial or short-lived perennial usually grown as a half-hardy annual – sow 3 mm (⅛ in) deep.

Olearia (Daisy Bush) Hardy and slightly tender evergreen shrubs – in late summer take 10 cm (4 in) long half-ripe cuttings and insert in pots placed in a cold frame.

Onopordum acanthium (Cotton Thistle, Scotch Thistle) Short-lived perennial usually grown as a hardy biennial – sow seeds 6 mm (¼ in) deep.

Origanum majorana (Knotted Marjoram, Sweet Marjoram) Slightly tender perennial usually grown as a half-hardy annual – during late winter and early spring sow seeds 3 mm (⅛ in) deep in pots placed in gentle warmth. Alternatively, during mid- and late spring sow seeds 6 mm (¼ in) deep outdoors.

Orontium aquaticum (Golden Club) Hardy aquatic – in spring and early summer lift and divide congested plants.

Osmanthus Hardy evergreen shrubs – in autumn layer low-growing stems. Alternatively, during mid-summer take 10 cm (4 in) long half-ripe cuttings and insert in pots placed in gentle warmth.

Osmunda regalis (Flowering Fern, Royal Fern) Hardy deciduous fern – in spring lift and divide congested clumps.

Osteospermum ecklonis var. prostratum Slightly tender bushy perennial – during mid-summer take 5 cm (2 in) long cuttings from sideshoots and insert in pots placed in a cold frame.

Pachysandra terminalis (Japanese Spurge) Hardy sprawling and ground-covering evergreen shrub – in early and mid-spring lift and divide congested plants.

Paeonia delavayi var. lutea Deciduous shrub – during early spring layer low-growing shoots. Alternatively, in autumn take 15–23 cm (6–9 in) long hardwood cuttings and insert in a cold frame or sheltered nursery bed.

A–Z OF PROPAGATING PLANTS

P   **P**

Paeonia lactiflora Herbaceous perennial – during early autumn lift and divide congested plants; ensure that each new piece has dormant buds and roots.

Paeonia lobata See *Paeonia peregrina*.

Paeonia lutea See *Paeonia delavayi* var. *lutea*.

Paeonia moutan See *Paeonia suffruticosa*.

Paeonia officinalis Herbaceous perennial – during early autumn lift and divide congested plants; ensure that each new piece has dormant buds and roots.

Paeonia peregrina Herbaceous perennial – during early autumn lift and divide congested plants; ensure that each new piece has dormant buds and roots.

Paeonia suffruticosa

Paeonia suffruticosa Deciduous shrub – during early spring layer low-growing shoots. Alternatively, in autumn take 15–23 cm (6–9 in) long hardwood cuttings and insert in a cold frame or sheltered nursery bed.

Papaver orientale (Oriental Poppy) Hardy herbaceous perennial – during spring lift and divide congested plants. Alternatively, during winter take root cuttings and insert in pots placed in a cold frame.

Papaver rhoeas (Field Poppy) Hardy annual – sow 6 mm (¼ in) deep.

Papaver somniferum (Opium Poppy) Hardy annual – sow seeds 6 mm (¼ in) deep.

Parrotia persica Hardy deciduous tree – in autumn layer low-growing stems. Alternatively, during late summer or autumn sow seeds in pots and place in a cold frame.

Parthenocissus henryana (Chinese Virginia Creeper) Hardy deciduous climber – in late summer take 10 cm (4 in) long cuttings from the current season's shoots and insert in pots placed in gentle warmth.

Parthenocissus tricuspidata (Boston Ivy) Hardy deciduous climber – in late summer take 10 cm (4 in) long cuttings from the current season's shoots and insert in pots placed in gentle warmth.

Passiflora (Passion Flower) Slightly tender evergreen climbers – during mid- and late summer take 7.5–10 cm (3–4 in) long cuttings and insert in pots placed in gentle warmth.

Pelargonium Tender sub-shrubs – during late summer and early autumn take 7.5 cm (3 in) long stem-tip cuttings and insert in pots placed in a cool greenhouse (see page 21). Alternatively, raise plants from seeds sown in gentle warmth in late winter or early spring.

Pericallis x hybrida (Florist's Cineraria) Half-hardy greenhouse perennial – from spring to late summer sow seeds 3 mm (⅛ in) deep in pots placed in gentle warmth.

Pernettya mucronata See *Gaultheria mucronata*.

Perovskia atriplicifolia (Russian Sage) Hardy, deciduous shrubby perennial – during mid-summer take 7.5 cm (3 in) long heel cuttings and insert in equal parts moist peat and sharp sand. Place in a cold frame.

Persicaria bistorta 'Superba' (Bistort, Snakeweed) Hardy herbaceous perennial – lift and divide congested plants in autumn or spring.

Petroselinum crispum

Petroselinum crispum (Parsley) Hardy biennial – in spring and early summer sow in a seed bed outdoors.

Petunia x hybrida Half-hardy perennial grown as a half-hardy annual – sow thinly and lightly press seeds into the compost.

Phacelia campanularia (California Bluebell) Hardy annual – sow seeds 6 mm (¼ in) deep.

Philadelphus (Mock Orange) Hardy deciduous shrubs – during mid- and late summer take 10 cm (4 in) long half-ripe cuttings from the current season's growth and insert in pots placed in a cold frame. Alternatively, in autumn take 25–30 cm (10–12 in) long hardwood cuttings; insert them vertically 20 cm (8 in) deep in a nursery bed.

Philodendron scandens (Sweetheart Plant) Greenhouse or house plant – layer long stems.

Phlomis fruticosa (Jerusalem Sage) Hardy shrubby evergreen – during late summer and early autumn take 7.5–10 cm (3–4 in) long cuttings and insert in pots placed in a cold frame.

Phlomis russeliana Hardy herbaceous perennial – during autumn or spring lift and divide congested plants.

Phlomis samia Hardy herbaceous perennial – during autumn or spring lift and divide congested plants.

Phlox adsurgens Hardy tufted perennial – during mid-summer take 5 cm (2 in) long basal cuttings and insert in pots placed in a cold frame.

Phlox douglasii Hardy sub-shrubby species – during mid-summer take 5 cm (2 in) long basal cuttings and insert in pots placed in a cold frame.

Phlox drummondii (Annual Phlox) Half-hardy annual – sow 6 mm (¼ in) deep.

Phlox maculata (Meadow Phlox, Wild Sweet William) Hardy herbaceous perennial – during autumn or spring lift and divide congested plants.

Phlox paniculata (Perennial Phlox, Summer Phlox) Hardy herbaceous perennial – during autumn or early spring lift and divide congested plants. Alternatively, take root cuttings.

Phlox subulata (Moss Phlox, Moss Pink) Hardy sub-shrubby species – during mid-summer take 5 cm (2 in) long basal cuttings; insert in pots in a cold frame.

Phormium tenax (New Zealand Flax, New Zealand Hemp) Half-hardy evergreen shrub – during spring lift and divide congested clumps. Ensure that each new plant has three or four leaves. Alternatively, new plants can be raised from seeds, but plants may not resemble the parents.

Physostegia virginiana (Obedient Plant) Hardy herbaceous perennial – during autumn or spring lift and divide congested plants.

Picea (Spruce, Fir) Hardy evergreen conifers – during spring sow seeds in pots and place in a cold frame.

Pieris Hardy evergreen shrubs – during late summer take 7.5–10 cm (3–4 in) long half-ripe cuttings and insert in pots placed in a cold frame. Alternatively, during late autumn or spring sow seeds in pots placed in a cold frame. Also, layer low-growing stems in autumn.

Pimpinella anisum (Aniseed) Hardy annual – sow 6 mm (¼ in) deep.

Pinus (Pine) Hardy evergreen conifers – in spring sow seeds in pots and place in a cold frame. However, varieties and named forms do not come true from seeds.

Piptanthus laburnifolius See *Piptanthus nepalensis*.

Piptanthus nepalensis Layer low branches in early autumn. Alternatively, sow seeds in pots in spring and place in a cold frame; or take 7.5–10 cm (3–4 in) long half-ripe heel cuttings in mid- and late summer and place in a cold frame.

Pittosporum tenuifolium

Pittosporum tenuifolium Slightly tender evergreen shrub or small tree – during mid-summer take 7.5–10 cm (3–4 in) long half-ripe heel cuttings and insert in pots placed in gentle warmth.

Platycodon grandiflorus (Balloon Flower) Hardy herbaceous perennial – during spring lift and divide congested plants.

Plectranthus coleoides 'Marginatus' (Swedish Ivy) Layer long stems.

Polemonium Hardy herbaceous perennials – during autumn or spring lift and divide congested plants.

Polygonatum x hybridum (David's Harp, Solomon's Seal) Hardy herbaceous perennial – lift and divide congested plants in autumn or spring.

Polygonum affine Hardy herbaceous perennial – lift and divide congested plants in autumn or spring.

Polygonum baldschuanicum See *Fallopia baldschuanica*.

Polygonum bistorta 'Superbum' See *Persicaria bistorta* 'Superba'.

Pontederia cordata (Pickerel Plant) Hardy herbaceous perennial – in late spring lift and divide congested plants.

Portulaca grandiflora (Sun Plant) Half-hardy annual – sow 3 mm (⅛ in) deep.

Potentilla atrosanguinea Hybrids Hardy herbaceous perennials – lift and divide congested plants in autumn or spring.

Potentilla fruticosa (Shrubby Cinquefoil) Bushy, deciduous shrub – take 7.5 cm (3 in) long cuttings from the current season's shoots in late summer; insert in equal parts moist peat and sharp sand and place in a cold frame.

Primula Range of hardy and half-hardy perennials, some grown indoors in temperate climates and others outdoors.

Indoor primulas

• **P. kewensis** Greenhouse perennial – during late spring and early summer sow seeds in pots placed in a cold frame or cool greenhouse. Barely cover the seeds.

• **P. malacoides** (Fairy Primrose) Greenhouse perennial usually grown as a greenhouse annual – from late spring to mid-summer sow seeds in pot placed in a cold frame or cool greenhouse. Barely cover the seeds.

A–Z OF PROPAGATING PLANTS

- **P. obconica** Greenhouse perennial usually grown as an annual – from spring to early summer sow seeds 3 mm (⅛ in) deep in pots placed in gentle warmth.

- **P. sinensis** Greenhouse perennial usually grown as a greenhouse annual – during late spring and early summer sow seeds in pots placed in a cold frame or cool greenhouse. Barely cover the seeds.

Hardy outdoor primulas

- **P. denticulata** (Drumstick Primula) Hardy perennial – during spring sow seeds in pots placed in a cold frame. Barely cover the seeds. Alternatively, take root cuttings.

- **P. florindae** (Giant Cowslip) Hardy perennial – during spring sow seeds in pots placed in a cold frame. Barely cover the seeds.

- **P. japonica** (Japanese Primrose) Hardy perennial – during spring sow seeds in pots placed in a cold frame. Barely cover the seeds.

- **P. Pruhonicensis Hybrids** (Polyanthus) Hardy perennial – in late winter and early spring sow seeds 3 mm (⅛ in) deep in pots and place in gentle warmth. Alternatively, sow seeds during late spring in a seed bed outdoors.

- **P. pulverulenta** Hardy perennial – during spring sow seeds in pots and place in a cold frame. Barely cover the seeds.

- **P. rosea** Hardy perennial – during spring sow seeds in pots and place in a cold frame. Barely cover the seeds.

- **P. vialii** Hardy perennial – during spring sow seeds shallowly in pots placed in a cold frame.

- **P. vulgaris** (Primrose) Hardy perennial – during late winter and early spring sow seeds 3 mm (⅛ in) deep in pots and place in gentle warmth. Alternatively, sow seeds during late spring and early summer in a seed bed outdoors.

Prunella (Self-heal) Hardy herbaceous perennials – during autumn or spring lift and divide congested plants.

Prunus, Almonds Hardy deciduous trees – bud onto selected rootstocks.

Prunus, Apricots Hardy deciduous trees – bud onto selected rootstocks.

Cherry

Prunus, Cherries Hardy deciduous trees – bud onto selected rootstocks.

Prunus, Damsons Hardy deciduous trees – bud onto selected rootstocks.

Prunus, Gages Hardy deciduous trees – bud onto selected rootstocks.

Prunus, Japanese Cherries Hardy deciduous trees and shrubs – during spring bud onto stocks of *P. avium* (Gean).

Prunus, Nectarines Hardy deciduous trees – bud onto selected rootstocks.

Prunus, Peaches Hardy deciduous trees – bud onto selected rootstocks.

Prunus, Plums Hardy deciduous trees – bud onto selected rootstocks.

Prunus cerasifera (Cherry Plum) Hardy deciduous tree – during mid-summer take 7.5–10 cm (3–4 in) long half-ripe cuttings and insert in pots in gentle warmth. Alternatively, layer low-growing stems in spring.

Prunus glandulosa Hardy dwarf and bushy shrub – layer low-growing shoots in spring.

Prunus incisa (Fuji Cherry) Hardy deciduous tree with a shrubby habit – during mid-summer take 7.5–10 cm (3–4 in) long half-ripe cuttings and insert in pots in gentle warmth.

Prunus laurocerasus (Cherry Laurel, Common Laurel) Evergreen shrub – during late summer or early autumn take 7.5–10 cm (3–4 in) long heel cuttings and insert in pots in a cold frame.

Prunus lusitanica (Portugal Laurel) Evergreen shrub – during late summer or early autumn take 7.5–10 cm (3–4 in) long heel cuttings and insert in pots in a cold frame.

Prunus padus (Bird Cherry) Hardy deciduous tree – during spring layer low branches.

Prunus spinosa (Sloe, Blackthorn) Hardy deciduous suckering shrub – during mid-summer take 7.5–10 cm (3–4 in) long half-ripe cuttings and insert in pots in gentle warmth.

Prunus subhirtella Hardy deciduous tree – during mid-summer take 7.5–10 cm (3–4 in) long half-ripe cuttings and insert in pots in gentle warmth.

Prunus tenella (Dwarf Russian Almond) Hardy deciduous shrub – during autumn remove and replant sucker-like shoots.

Pulmonaria officinalis (Blue Lungwort, Jerusalem Cowslip) Hardy herbaceous perennial – lift and divide congested plants in autumn or spring.

Pulsatilla vulgaris (Pasque Flower) Hardy herbaceous perennial – during mid-summer sow seeds in pots placed in a cold frame.

Pyracantha

Pyracantha (Firethorn) Hardy evergreen shrubs – during mid- and late summer take 7.5–10 cm (3–4 in) long cuttings inserted in pots placed in gentle warmth.

Pyrethrum roseum See *Tanacetum coccineum.*

Ramonda myconi Rosette-forming rock garden evergreen – during early and mid-summer take leaf cuttings. Remove a leaf from the plant (ensuring a bud remains at its base) and insert at a slight angle in a pot. Place in a cold frame.

Ramonda pyrenaica See *Ramonda myconi.*

Reseda odorata (Mignonette) Hardy annual – sow 3 mm (⅛ in) deep.

Rhododendron Mainly hardy deciduous and evergreen shrubs and trees:

• **Deciduous azaleas** – use grafting or layering.

• **Evergreen azaleas** – take cuttings in mid- or late summer and insert in pots placed in a cold frame.

• **Large-leaved species** – layer low-growing stems at any time. Alternatively, sow seeds during late winter and early spring in pots placed in gentle warmth.

• **Hardy hybrids** – take cuttings, or graft.

Rhus typhina (Stag's Horn Sumach) Hardy deciduous shrub – during spring layer low-growing shoots. Some *Rhus* species produce sucker-like growths and these can be removed during autumn or spring and planted into their growing positions. Alternatively, during mid- and late summer take 10–13 cm (4–5 in) long heel cuttings and insert in pots placed in gentle warmth; or take root cuttings.

Ribes (Flowering Currant) Hardy and half-hardy evergreen and deciduous shrubs:

• **Deciduous species** – during autumn take 25 cm (10 in) long hardwood cuttings and insert in a nursery bed.

• **Evergreen species** (Ribes laurifolium) – during early autumn take 7.5–10 cm (3–4 in) long cuttings and insert in pots placed in a cold frame.

Rodgersia Hardy herbaceous species – during spring lift and divide congested plants.

Romneya coulteri (Californian Tree Poppy, Matilija, Tree Poppy) Hardy semi-woody shrub with herbaceous-like stems – during late winter or early spring sow seeds 3–6 mm (⅛– ¼ in) deep in pots placed in gentle warmth. Alternatively, take 7.5 cm (3 in) long root cuttings in late winter and place in gentle warmth. Sometimes, sucker-like shoots arise from the bases of disturbed shrubs and these can be dug up and replanted in spring.

Rosa (Roses) Hardy deciduous shrubs and climbers – raised from seeds, cuttings and by budding:

• **Seeds** – only species come true from seeds, and then only if pollinated by hand.

• **Cuttings** – best reserved for miniature roses, shrub roses, true species and their hybrids, and some ramblers.

• **Budding** – mainly used for Hybrid Tea and Floribunda roses.

Rosmarinus officinalis (Rosemary) Hardy evergreen shrub – during mid-summer take 7.5–10 cm (3–4 in) long cuttings and insert in pots placed in a cold frame.

Rubus (Ornamental Brambles) Hardy, erect or scrambling, evergreen and deciduous shrubs – in autumn or early spring lift and divide congested clumps. Alternatively, in late summer or early autumn take semi-hardwood 7.5–10 cm (3–4 in) long cuttings and insert in pots placed in a cold frame.

Rudbeckia fulgida (Coneflower) Hardy herbaceous perennial – in autumn or spring lift and divide congested plants.

Rudbeckia hirta (Black-eyed Susan, Coneflower) Hardy annual – sow 6 mm (¼ in) deep. Alternatively, raise as a half-hardy annual – sow 3 mm (⅛ in) deep.

Ruta graveolens (Rue) Hardy evergreen shrub – during late summer take 7.5–10 cm (3–4 in) long cuttings from lateral shoots and insert in pots placed in a cold frame. Alternatively, raise from seeds.

Saintpaulia ionantha (African Violet) Greenhouse or house plant – from early summer to early autumn take leaf cuttings and insert in pots placed in gentle warmth. Alternatively, root leaf-petiole cuttings in water or compost (see pages 21 and 25) or divide (see page 31).

Salix (Willow) Hardy deciduous trees and shrubs – from mid-autumn to early spring take 23–38 cm (9–15 in) long hardwood cuttings. Insert them vertically in a nursery bed.

Salpiglossis sinuata (Painted Tongue) Half-hardy annual – sow 3 mm (⅛ in) deep.

Salvia horminum See *Salvia viridus.*

Salvia officinalis (Sage) Relatively short-lived, evergreen, tender shrub – during late summer take 7.5 cm (3 in) long heel cuttings and insert in pots placed in a cold frame.

Salvia patens Half-hardy perennial usually grown as a half-hardy annual – sow 6 mm (¼ in) deep.

Salvia sclarea (Clary) Hardy biennial usually grown as an annual – sow 6 mm (¼ in) deep.

Salvia splendens (Scarlet Sage) Half-hardy perennial usually grown as a half-hardy annual – sow 6 mm (¼ in) deep.

Salvia viridus Hardy annual – sow 6 mm (¼ in) deep.

Sambucus (Elder) Hardy deciduous shrubs and small trees – during late autumn take 25–30 cm (10–12 in) long hardwood cuttings and insert vertically in a nursery bed. Alternatively, during mid- and late summer take 10–13 cm (4–5 in) long half-ripe heel cuttings and insert in pots placed in a cold frame.

Sansevieria trifasciata (Mother-in-law's Tongue) Greenhouse or house plant – during summer detach sucker-like shoots from around plants and insert in pots placed in gentle warmth. Alternatively, take leaf cuttings (see page 27). Divide the yellow-edged form S. trifasciata var. laurentii (see page 31).

Santolina (Cotton Lavender) Hardy evergreen shrubs – from mid-summer to early autumn take 5–7.5 cm (2–3 in) long half-ripe cuttings from sideshoots and insert in pots placed in a cold frame.

Satureja hortensis (Summer Savory) Hardy annual – sow 6 mm (¼ in) deep.

Satureja montana (Winter Savory) Hardy and almost evergreen perennial – raise as a hardy annual. Alternatively, during spring take 5 cm (2 in) long cuttings from lateral shoots and insert in pots placed in a cold frame. Additionally, lift and divide congested plants in spring.

Saxifraga Wide range of plants, mostly hardy and forming rosettes – during late spring and early summer detach non-flowering rosettes and insert in pots placed in a cold frame.

Saxifraga sarmentosa See Saxifraga stolonifera.

Saxifraga stolonifera (Mother of Thousands, Strawberry Geranium) Tender perennial, often grown indoors or in hanging-baskets – during early summer detach young rosettes, insert in compost and place in gentle warmth. Alternatively, place parent plant in a central position and peg the rosettes into pots of compost. Detach stems when rooted.

Scabiosa atropurpurea (Sweet Scabious) Hardy annual – sow 12 mm (½ in) deep.

Schefflera actinophylla (Umbrella Tree) Greenhouse or house plant – during late winter and early spring sow seeds in pots placed in gentle warmth.

Schefflera arboricola (Parasol Plant) Greenhouse or house plant – during late winter and early spring sow seeds in pots placed in gentle warmth.

Schefflera elegantissima (False Aralia) Greenhouse or house plant – during spring sow seeds in pots placed in gentle warmth. Alternatively, take stem cuttings in spring – but rooting is difficult.

Schizanthus pinnatus (Butterfly Flower, Poor Man's Orchid) Half-hardy annual – sow 3 mm (⅛ in) deep.

Schizophragma Hardy deciduous climbers – during mid- and late summer take 7.5–10 cm (3–4 in) long half-ripe cuttings and insert in pots placed in gentle warmth. Alternatively, layer low-growing shoots in autumn.

Schizostylis Slightly tender herbaceous perennials – during spring lift and divide congested plants.

Scilla (Squill) Hardy bulb – lift and divide congested clumps as the leaves die down. Divide them and replant immediately.

Sedum 'Autumn Joy' Hardy herbaceous perennial – lift and divide congested plants in autumn or spring.

Sedum 'Herbstfreude' – see Sedum 'Autumn Joy'.

Sedum sieboldii Greenhouse or house plant – remove and root small leaves.

Sedum sieboldii 'Mediovariegatum' Greenhouse or house plant – remove and root small leaves.

Sempervivum

Sempervivum (Houseleek) Hardy and half-hardy rosette-forming evergreen succulents – during spring detach rooted offsets and either plant directly into their growing positions or, if small, into pots placed in a cold frame. Alternatively, during early spring sow seeds in pots placed in a cold frame.

Senecio bicolor See Senecio cineraria.

Senecio cineraria Half-hardy perennial, raised in a greenhouse in spring – sow 3 mm (⅛ in) deep.

Senecio cruentus See Pericallis x hybrida.

Senecio x hybridus See Pericallis x hybrida.

Senecio macroglossus 'Variegatus' (Cape Ivy, Wax Ivy) Greenhouse or house plant – take stem cuttings.

Senecio maritimus See Senecio cineraria.

Senecio 'Sunshine' See *Brachyglottis* 'Sunshine'.

Setcreasea pallida See *Tradescantia pallida.*

Sidalcea malviflora (Checkerbloom) Hardy herbaceous perennial – lift and divide congested clumps in spring.

Sinningia speciosa (Gloxinia) Greenhouse or house plant – take and root cross-sections of leaves.

Sisyrinchium Hardy herbaceous perennials – during autumn or spring lift and divide congested plants. Alternatively, during autumn or spring sow seeds in pots placed in a cold frame.

Solanum crispum (Chilean Potato Tree) Slightly tender semi-evergreen climber – during mid- and late summer take 7.5–10 cm (3–4 in) long cuttings from sideshoots and insert in pots placed in gentle warmth.

Solanum jasminoides See *Solanum laxum.*

Solanum laxum (Jasmine Nightshade) Tender semi-evergreen climber – during mid- and late summer take 7.5–10 cm (3–4 in) long cuttings from sideshoots and insert in pots placed in gentle warmth.

Solenostemon scutellarioides (Coleus, Flame Nettle, Painted Nettle) Greenhouse perennial – sow 3 mm (⅛ in) deep.

Solidago hybrids (Golden Rod) Hardy herbaceous perennial – lift and divide congested plants during autumn or spring.

Spartium junceum (Spanish Broom) Hardy deciduous shrub – during early and mid-spring sow seeds in pots placed in a cold frame.

Spathiphyllum wallisii (Peace Lily) Greenhouse or house plant – during spring divide congested plants (see page 31).

Spiraea 'Arguta' (Bridal Wreath, Foam of May) Hardy deciduous shrub – in mid-summer take 7.5–10 cm (3–4 in) long cuttings from the current season's shoots. Insert them in pots and place in a cold frame.

Spiraea x bumalda See *Spiraea japonica* 'Bumalda'.

Spiraea japonica Hardy deciduous shrub – during autumn or spring divide congested plants. In mid-summer take 7.5–10 cm (3–4 in) long cuttings from the current season's shoots. Insert them in pots and place in a cold frame.

Spiraea japonica 'Bumalda' Hardy deciduous shrub – during autumn or spring divide congested plants. In mid-summer take 7.5–10 cm (3–4 in) long cuttings from the current season's shoots. Insert them in pots and place in a cold frame.

Spiraea thunbergii Hardy deciduous shrub – in mid-summer take 7.5–10 cm (3–4 in) long cuttings from the current season's shoots. Insert them in pots and place in a cold frame.

Stachys byzantina (Lamb's Ears, Lamb's Tongue) Half-hardy herbaceous perennial – lift and divide congested plants in autumn or spring.

Stachys lanata See *Stachys byzantina.*

Stachys olympica See *Stachys byzantina.*

Stenotaphrum secundatum (Buffalo Grass) Greenhouse or house plant – divide congested plants.

Stenotaphrum secundatum 'Variegatum' (Variegated Buffalo Grass) Greenhouse or house plant – divide congested plants.

Streptocarpus x hybridus (Cape Primrose) Greenhouse or house plant – from late spring to mid-summer take leaf cuttings; insert in wide pots and place in gentle warmth. Alternatively, during spring divide congested plants.

Symphoricarpos (Snowberry) Hardy deciduous shrubs – during autumn or spring remove rooted stems and replant into their growing positions or a nursery bed. Alternatively, in autumn or late winter take 20–25 cm (8–10 in) long hardwood cuttings and insert in a nursery bed.

Symphytum grandiflorum (Comfrey) Hardy herbaceous perennial – lift and divide congested plants in autumn or spring.

Syringa x chinensis Hardy deciduous shrub – during mid-summer take 7.5 cm (3 in) long half-ripe heel cuttings and insert in pots placed in a cold frame.

Syringa meyeri 'Palibin' Hardy deciduous shrub – during mid-summer take 7.5 cm (3 in) long half-ripe heel cuttings and insert in pots placed in a cold frame.

Syringa pubescens subsp. microphylla 'Superba' Hardy deciduous shrub – during mid-summer take 7.5 cm (3 in) long half-ripe heel cuttings and insert in pots placed in a cold frame.

Syringa vulgaris

Syringa vulgaris (Common Lilac) Hardy deciduous shrub or small tree – varieties are budded during mid-summer to ensure progeny resemble the parent plant. Alternatively, in mid-summer take 7.5 cm (3 in) long half-ripe heel cuttings and insert in pots placed in a cold frame.

A-Z OF PROPAGATING PLANTS

T **V**

Tagetes erecta (African Marigold)
Half-hardy annual – sow 6 mm (¼ in) deep.

Tagetes patula (French Marigold)
Half-hardy annual – sow 6 mm (¼ in) deep.

Tagetes tenuifolia (Signet Marigold)
Half-hardy annual – sow 6 mm (¼ in) deep.

Tamarix (Tamarisk) Hardy deciduous
shrubs – in autumn take 23–25 cm (9–10
in) long hardwood cuttings and insert in a
nursery bed.

Tanacetum coccineum Hardy
herbaceous perennial – sow 6 mm (¼ in)
deep. Alternatively, during early spring lift
and divide congested plants.

Tanacetum parthenium
(Feverfew) Hardy, short-lived perennial
usually grown as a half-hardy annual – sow
3 mm (⅛ in) in deep.

Tanacetum ptarmiciflorum
(Silver Lace) Half-hardy perennial usually
grown as a half-hardy annual – sow 6 mm
(¼ in) deep.

Tanacetum vulgare (Tansy) Hardy
perennial – during autumn or spring lift
and divide congested plants.

Taxodium distichum (Bald Cypress,
Swamp Cypress) Hardy deciduous conifer
– during spring sow seeds in pots placed in
a cold frame.

Taxus baccata (Yew) Hardy
evergreen conifer – in late summer take
7.5 cm (3 in) long heel cuttings and insert
in pots in a cold frame.

Thalictrum aquilegiifolium
(Meadow Rue) Hardy herbaceous
perennial – lift and divide congested plants
in spring.

Thuja plicata (Western Red Cedar)
Hardy evergreen conifer – in late summer
take 7.5 cm (3 in) long cuttings from the
tips of shoots and insert in pots placed in a
cold frame.

Thunbergia alata (Black-eyed Susan)
Half-hardy annual – sow 6 mm (¼ in) deep.

Thymus (Thyme) Hardy evergreen
carpeting shrub – during spring or late
summer lift and divide congested plants.
Alternatively, in mid-summer take 5 cm
(2 in) long heel cuttings and insert in pots
placed in a cold frame.

Tiarella cordifolia (Foam Flower)
Hardy, ground-covering perennial – divide
congested plants in autumn or spring.

Tiarella wherryi Hardy, ground-
covering perennial – sow 3–6 mm (⅛–
¼ in) deep in pots in spring and place in
a cold frame.

Tolmiea menziesii (Pick-a-back
Plant, Youth-on-age) Hardy evergreen
perennial grown outdoors or as a house
plant – detach leaves bearing plantlets and
peg them on the compost's surface. Later,
detach rooted plantlets and transfer singly
into pots.

Trachelium caeruleum (Blue Lace
Flower, Queen Anne's Lace) Hardy
biennial often grown as a half-hardy annual
– sow 3 mm (⅛ in) deep.

Trachelospermum Hardy evergreen
climbing shrubs – during mid- and late
summer take 7.5–10 cm (3–4 in) long
cuttings from sideshoots and insert in pots
placed in gentle warmth.

Trachycarpus fortunei (Chinese
Windmill Palm, Chusan Palm) Evergreen
palm – in late spring cut off large suckers
from around the plant's base and pot up
into loam-based compost. Place in gentle
warmth until rooted, then transfer to
nursery bed.

Tradescantia albiflora See
Tradescantia fluminensis.

Tradescantia x andersoniana
(Spiderwort, Trinity Flower) Hardy
herbaceous perennial – lift and divide
congested plants in spring.

Tradescantia fluminensis
(Wandering Jew) Greenhouse or house
plant – from late spring to early autumn
insert stem-tip cuttings in pots and place in
gentle warmth.

Tradescantia pallida Greenhouse
or house plant – during summer take
7.5–10 cm (3–4 in) long basal cuttings and
insert in pots placed in gentle warmth.

Tradescantia virginiana Hardy
herbaceous perennial – lift and divide
congested plants in spring.

Trillium Hardy rhizomatous-rooted
perennials – lift and divide congested
clumps when the leaves have died down
(in late summer) and until early spring.

Trollius x cultorum (Globe Flower)
Hardy herbaceous perennial – lift and
divide congested plants in autumn or
spring.

Tropaeolum majus (Nasturtium)
Hardy annual – sow 12 mm (½ in) deep.

Tropaeolum peregrinum (Canary
Creeper) Half-hardy perennial often
grown as a hardy annual – sow seeds
12 mm (½ in) deep. Alternatively, treat as a
half-hardy annual – sow seeds 12 mm
(½ in) deep.

Tropaeolum speciosum (Flame
Flower) Hardy deciduous perennial
climber – in spring divide congested plants.

Tulipa (Tulip) Hardy bulbs – lift bulbs as
soon as the flowers fade and put them in a
dry, vermin-free shed. When the stems and
leaves have died, place the bulbs in dry
boxes and store in a dry, airy shed until
autumn. Break up large clusters of bulbs.

Ulex europaeus (Gorse) Hardy
evergreen spiny shrub – during late
summer and early autumn take 7.5 cm
(3 in) long cuttings and insert in pots
placed in a cold frame. Alternatively, sow
seeds in mid-spring in pots in a cold frame.

Ursinia anethoides Half-hardy
perennial often grown as a half-hardy
annual – sow 3 mm (⅛ in) deep.

Verbascum blattaria (Moth
Mullein) Hardy biennial – during spring
sow seeds in pots placed in a cold frame.
Alternatively, take root cuttings.

Verbascum bombyciferum Hardy biennial – during spring sow seeds in pots placed in a cold frame. Alternatively, take root cuttings.

Verbascum densiflorum (Large-flowered Mullein) Hardy perennial usually grown as a hardy biennial – during spring sow seeds in pots placed in a cold frame. Alternatively, take root cuttings.

Verbascum dumulosum Sub-shrubby perennial – during early and mid-summer take 5 cm (2 in) long heel cuttings and insert in pots placed in a cold frame. Alternatively, take root cuttings.

Verbascum 'Letitia' Hardy bushlet – during early and mid-summer take 5 cm (2 in) long heel cuttings and insert in pots placed in a cold frame. Alternatively, take root cuttings.

Verbascum phlomoides (Woolly Mullein) Hardy biennial – during spring, sow seeds in pots placed in a cold frame. Alternatively, take root cuttings.

Verbascum phoeniceum (Purple Mullein) Hardy perennial or biennial – during spring sow seeds in pots placed in a cold frame. Alternatively, raise as a half-hardy annual; or take root cuttings.

Verbascum spinosum Sub-shrubby perennial – during early and mid-summer take 5 cm (2 in) long heel cuttings and insert in pots placed in a cold frame. Alternatively, take root cuttings.

Verbascum thapsiforme See *Verbascum densiflorum.*

Verbascum thapsus (Aaron's Rod, Common Mullein) Hardy biennial – during spring sow seeds in pots placed in a cold frame. Alternatively, take root cuttings.

Verbena See *Verbena* x *hybrida.*

Verbena x hybrida (Verbena) Half-hardy perennial usually grown as a half-hardy annual – sow 3 mm (⅛ in) deep.

Veronica (Speedwell) Wide range of plants including annuals and herbaceous perennials for rock gardens and borders. During spring lift and divide herbaceous border types. During mid- and late summer take 5 cm (2 in) long cuttings from lateral shoots of rock garden species. Non-invasive types can be divided in spring.

Viburnum Hardy deciduous and evergreen shrubs – during mid-summer take 7.5–10 cm (3–4 in) long cuttings, preferably with a heel, from the current season's shoots. Insert them in pots of equal parts moist peat and sharp sand and place in gentle warmth. Alternatively, layer low-growing shoots in late summer.

Vinca major (Greater Periwinkle) Hardy, sprawling evergreen shrub – trailing stems naturally root into the soil and can be detached in spring. Alternatively, lift and divide congested plants in autumn or spring; replant in their growing positions.

Vinca minor (Lesser Periwinkle) Hardy, sprawling evergreen shrub – trailing stems naturally root into the soil and can be detached in spring. Alternatively, lift and divide congested plants in autumn or spring; replant in their growing positions.

Viola x wittrockiana (Pansy) Hardy biennial – sow 6 mm (¼ in) deep.

Vitis coignetiae (Crimson Glory Vine, Japanese Crimson Glory Vine) Hardy deciduous climber – during autumn layer one-year-old stems.

Vitis vinifera (Grape Vine) Hardy deciduous climber – during mid- and late summer take 10–13 cm (4–5 in) long half-ripe heel cuttings and insert in pots in gentle warmth.

Weigela hybrids Hardy deciduous shrub – in autumn take 25–30 cm (10–12 in) long hardwood cuttings and insert vertically in a nursery bed.

Wisteria floribunda (Japanese Wisteria) Hardy deciduous climber – in mid-summer take 7.5–10 cm (3–4 in) long cuttings and insert in pots placed in gentle warmth.

Wisteria sinensis (Chinese Wisteria) Hardy deciduous climber – in mid-summer take 7.5–10 cm (3–4 in) long cuttings and insert in pots placed in gentle warmth. Additionally, layer low-growing shoots in late spring.

Xerochrysum bracteatum (Everlasting Flower) Half-hardy perennial raised as a half-hardy annual – sow 3 mm (⅛ in) deep. Alternatively, sow 6 mm (¼ in) deep in the open soil in spring where the plants are to grow and flower.

Yucca filamentosa (Adam's Needle) Slightly tender evergreen shrub – in spring cut off rooted suckers and plant directly in their growing positions. Small suckers can be planted in a nursery bed before being planted in a border. Alternatively, take cane cuttings.

Yucca gloriosa Slightly tender evergreen shrub – in spring cut off rooted suckers and plant directly into their growing positions. Small suckers can be planted into a nursery bed before being planted into a border. Alternatively, take cane cuttings.

Yucca recurvifolia Slightly tender evergreen shrub – in spring cut off rooted suckers and plant directly into their growing positions. Small suckers can be planted in a nursery bed before being planted in a border. Alternatively, take cane cuttings.

Zantedeschia aethiopica 'Crowborough' (Arum Lily, Calla Lily) Half-hardy, deciduous, rhizomatous-rooted perennial – lift and divide congested plants in spring.

Zinnia elegans Half-hardy annual – sow 6 mm (¼ in) deep. Alternatively, raise as a hardy annual – sow 6–12 mm (¼–½ in) deep.

Glossary

Air layering Method of encouraging roots to form on a stem. Often used on houseplants such as *Ficus elastica* (Rubber Plant).

Annual Plant that grows from seed, flowers and dies within the same growing season.

Anther The male part of a flower that produces pollen.

Asexual Non-sexual; often used to refer to increasing plants by vegetative methods, such as cuttings, division, grafting and budding.

Biennial Plant that initially makes its growth one year, flowers during the following year and then dies.

Bigeneric hybrid A plant produced by crossing two plants from different genera.

Bottom heat The warming of a rooting medium from below.

Budding Uniting a bud of a varietal part with a rootstock of known vigour and quality.

Bulbils Small, immature bulbs found around the bases of some bulbs. They can be detached, sown and encouraged to form roots. Some leaves also produce bulbils.

Cambium Tissue just beneath the bark of woody plant. When grafting, the cambium of both parts must unite.

Cane cuttings Stems (without leaves) that are severed from parent plants and either inserted vertically into compost or pressed into the surface of the compost.

Clone Plant raised vegetatively from another and therefore identical to it.

Compost Refers to the mixture in which cuttings are inserted, seeds are sown and plants repotted. Compost can also refer to decomposed vegetative material that is sometimes mixed into garden soil or used as a mulch.

Cutting Vegetative method of propagation; a shoot is detached from a parent plant and encouraged to form roots.

Dibber (dibble) Wooden or plastic tool for making a hole in soil in gardens (especially vegetable plots and nursery beds) and in compost in seed-trays (flats) and pots. Those used outdoors are 20–30 cm (8–12 in) long and usually with a T- or D-shaped handle. Those used in greenhouses are like fat pencils and 10–15 cm (4–6 in) long.

Division Vegetative method of propagation involving dividing roots.

Eye Growth bud on a tuber, or a bud on a stem.

Eye cuttings Method of increasing grape vines.

F1 The first filial generation, the result of a cross between two pure-bred parents.

Fertilization The sexual union of a male and female cell.

Fluid sowing Mixing seeds with a gel in a plastic bag and squeezing it along a drill. It helps seeds to remain moist before germination.

Gootee layering Also known as 'marcottage' and used to encourage roots to develop on stems, usually shrubs and trees.

Grafting The uniting of a varietal part with roots of known vigour.

Half-hardy annuals Plants raised early in gentle warmth and later planted outdoors when the weather improves and is free from frost.

Half-ripe cuttings Formed of semi-ripe shoots. Also known as semi-ripe cuttings and semi-mature cuttings.

Hardening off Slowly acclimatizing plants to outdoor conditions.

Hardy annuals Plants sown directly into their flowering positions outdoors.

Heel cutting Cutting, usually a half-ripe type, with part of a shoot attached to its base.

Hormone Chemical that influences the growth and development of plant. Hormone rooting-powders are often used to encourage cuttings to form roots.

Hybrid The progeny of parents of different species or genera.

Internode The length of a stem between two leaf-joints (nodes).

Inverted-L graft Type of graft used to rejuvenate old fruit trees.

Layering Encouraging stems to develop roots, either in a greenhouse or garden.

Leaf-petiole cutting Cutting formed of a leaf and its leaf stem.

Leaf squares Small squares, cut from a leaf, that can be encouraged to form roots.

Leaf-stem cutting Cutting formed of a piece of stem and leaf.

Leaf triangles Small triangles, cut from a leaf, that can be encouraged to form roots.

Marcottage Also known as 'gootee' layering and used to encourage the development of roots on stems, usually of trees and shrubs.

Mist propagation Method of regularly covering cuttings with a fine mist spray to keep them cool, reduce transpiration and to encourage rapid rooting.

Nicking Using a sharp knife to shallowly cut a seed's coat to encourage rapid germination.

Node The point at which leaves, stems and sideshoots arise. It is usually slightly swollen.

Petiole A leaf stem.

Plantlets Small, immature plants that develop on leaves or at the ends of stems.

Pollination The alighting of pollen (male part) on the stigma (female part) of a flower.

Pricking off The initial moving of seedlings from where they were sown into pots or seed-trays (flats).

Propagation Increasing plants.

Propagators Enclosed, plastic or glass-covered units in which seeds are encouraged to germinate and cuttings to form roots. Some are heated.

Rhizome Horizontal, creeping, underground or partly underground stem that acts as a storage organ. Can be divided to create new plants.

Root cuttings Way to increase plants by severing roots and placing them in compost.

Rootstock The roots upon which plants are grafted or budding.

Runner Shoot that grows along the ground, rooting and forming new plants.

Saddle grafting Method of grafting plants, especially rhododendrons.

Scion Shoot or bud that is grafted onto a rootstock.

Seed-tray Flat-based tray for sowing seeds and transplanting seedlings into. Known in North America as a flat.

Semi-hardwood cutting Another term for half-ripe cutting.

Semi-mature cutting Another term for half-ripe cutting.

Silver sand Very fine horticultural sand that has been cleaned.

Spore Spores are small bodies found on the undersides of fern fronds. To raise ferns from ripe (plump) spores, sow them on hot-water-sterilized compost, cover with clingfilm, place in gentle warmth and regularly mist-spray the surface.

Stool Usually means the roots of cut-down chrysanthemums. Also refers to some shrubs with masses of shoots that grow from ground level.

Strain Seed-raised plants from a common ancestor.

Stratification Subjecting seeds to a temperature change for a period of time to encourage germination.

Sucker Shoot that arises from below ground level, usually from roots but occasionally from stems.

Thinning Removing congested seedlings to leave healthy ones spaced out.

Ti-log cuttings Formed of stems (without leaves) and inserted vertically in compost to encourage the formation of roots.

Tip cutting Softwood cutting formed from a growing tip, piece of stem and a few leaves.

Tip-layering Encouraging the tips of shoots to develop roots.

Transplanting Moving young plants from a nursery bed to where they will grow and mature. The term is also used when established plants are moved.

Tuber Thickened, fleshy root (dahlia) or an underground stem (potato). These can be increased by division.

Vegetative Refers to propagation and includes methods of increasing plants by cuttings, layers, grafting, budding and division. Sowing seeds is not a vegetative method.

Whip-and-tongue grafting Used to create some fruit trees.

Index

Acknowledgments

AG&G Books would like to thank **Thompson & Morgan** for their contribution: Quality Seedsmen Since 1855, brings the finest quality *flower and vegetable seed and flower plant varieties to the home gardener,* Thompson & Morgan (UK) Ltd, Poplar Lane, Ipswich, Suffolk, IP8 3BU. Photographs: AG&G Books, David Squire (pages 4TL, 4BR, 5TL, 5TR, 10TL, 10TR, 10BR, 11TL and 11TR), Garden Matters (page 4BL) and Thompson & Morgan (pages 10BL and 11TC).